THE SPANIARDS
IN THEIR HISTORY

RAMÓN MENÉNDEZ PIDAL, the great patriarch of humanism in the Spanish world, has devoted his life to unravelling and explaining the history of medieval Spain. Born in Galicia in 1869, he is now, at the age of ninety-seven, still actively engaged in his studies. As a young man he was a philologist and spent many years studying the Spanish Epic and Romancero. In 1899 he became Profesor of Romance Philology at the University of Madrid. From 1926 to 1936 he was Director of the Royal Spanish Academy, and was reappointed to that position after the war in 1948.

Menéndez Pidal has published many works on Spanish culture, few of which have been translated. He has lectured in this country at Johns Hopkins and Columbia Universities.

Ramón Menéndez Pidal

THE SPANIARDS
IN THEIR HISTORY

Translated and with an introduction by
WALTER STARKIE

The Norton Library
W · W · NORTON & COMPANY · INC ·
NEW YORK

Books That Live
The Norton imprint on a book means that in the publisher's
estimation it is a book not for a single season but for the years.
W. W. Norton & Company, Inc.

ISBN   0   393   00353   1

456789

Contents

INTRODUCTION TO THE ESSAY ON SPAIN BY WALTER STARKIE   1

THE SPANIARDS IN THEIR HISTORY

I.	MATERIAL AND MORAL AUSTERITY	17
II.	IDEALISM	36
III.	INDIVIDUALISM	44
IV.	CENTRALIZATION AND REGIONALISM	75
V.	THE TWO SPAINS	102

MAPS

I.	Cultural Map of Spain in Roman Times and the Golden Age	144
II.	Christian and Moorish Kingdoms at the middle of the eleventh century	145
III.	The Mediaeval Kingdoms and different languages in the thirteenth century	145

BIBLIOGRAPHY   146

Introduction

The Essay on Spain

It is instructive to compare the essay of Menéndez Pidal with some of the essays on Spain by his contemporaries. First of all, let us consider '*Psicología del Pueblo Español*' by the eminent historian Rafael Altamira which was published in 1902, and republished in 1917. Altamira describes in the preface how he wrote his book in the summer of 1898, when Spain sustained her tragic war with the United States of America. In the atmosphere of gloom, amidst the tears of some, the indignation of others, and the passive indifference of the majority he wrote feverishly in an attempt to raise the morale of his countrymen, for he hoped against hope that a movement of regeneration would come to Spain as it had come to Prussia in 1808, leading to the victorious Germany of 1870. What he longed for was a movement of regeneration which would correct national defects and inject fresh vigour into the body politic, and rescue the country from the deep decadence into which it had sunk. As a result, Altamira produced a description of the Spanish character which is a useful compendium for one reading the authors of the 1898 movement. After quoting the opinions of the eighteenth-century masters, such as Masdeu and Feijóo, he devotes attention to Ganivet, whose tragic death seemed to foreshadow the national disaster. It was Ganivet who explained the essence of the Spanish conception of justice. The Spaniard aspires to pure and absolute justice, and he insists that it should be rigorous, even implacable. But at the same time the Spaniard is always ready to pity the fallen, and he will take as much trouble to raise him up as he did to overthrow him. This characteristic, according to Ganivet, sprang from the stoicism of Seneca, and was a genuine Spanish trait. In considering the eighteenth century Altamira remarks that no

1

historian has adequately studied the causes of the decline of Spain in the last years of Charles IV, and later, when the country after the War of Independence neglected intellectual pursuits and fell into the obscurantism of Ferdinand VII's reign, thus preparing the ground for the troubled years of Isabel II. Let us not forget, he says, that Spain is the European nation which has suffered the greatest number of years of war in the nineteenth century. Up to 1896 Spain had sustained thirty-one years of war; France twenty-seven; Russia twenty-four; Italy twenty-three; England twenty-one, and Germany thirteen, but the majority of these wars were not civil but international.[1]

Altamira began to write his book in the tragic days of 1898, and in the succeeding years he analyses the various pessimistic writers who devoted their attention to the complex problems of Spanish decadence. One writer after another pointed out the defects of the Spanish character. Macías Picavea for instance in '*El Problema Nacional*' described Spain as an ailing country, whose defects were immeasurably greater than her virtues, and those vices which had atrophied the organs of her national life sprang from the Caesarism, despotism, caciquism, theocracy, and Catholic intolerance which came in with the House of Austria. Macías saw no hope in the masses or in collective effort. There was only one solution: Spain would have to discover 'a man', that is to say, a genius; one of those benevolent dictators who can change the destiny of a nation. When Altamira published his book in 1902 the new literary movement of 1898 was already well under way. Azorín was already awakening the Spaniards and making them observe the world around them and discover beauties in the tiny pueblos that lie strewn like toys on the Meseta of Castile. Unamuno, with his Quixotism and his gospel of struggle and agony, was turning men's minds, not only to Tertullian and Augustine, but also to the Danish philosopher Kirkegaard: Baroja was revolutionizing the Spanish novel and creating a modern kind of picaresque narration. When Altamira published the second edition of his book in 1917 he found himself obliged to vary his text in places and add an extra chapter on actual psychological characteristics. In the new preface he refers to the great mass of literature written by the Hispanophobes as a

[1] R. Altamira, *Psicología del Pueblo Español*, 2nd ed., Madrid, 1917, p. 152.

result of the political passions aroused by the wars of Italy against Spanish domination, the conflict for hegemony between France and Spain, the religious wars, the struggle for independence in the Netherlands, and finally the American question in which Dutch, English and French took part. That literature makes quaint reading to-day, for in it we find Spanish psychology treated by the Hispanophobes in a special way for political reasons. This gave rise on the part of the Spaniards, the partisans of the House of Austria, and Catholics in general, to a series of counter-works defending Spanish history and the character or psychology of the people. This conflict which was acute in the eighteenth century died down in the nineteenth century, but the legendary tales of travellers and the fantastic description of Spanish life did not cease, and there arose the struggle between the Liberals and the Reactionaries, to which I referred in my description of Menéndez Pelayo. At the end of the century the dispute again became international on the occasion of the Cuban War, when Hispanophobia was exploited by the jingoist press of the United States.[1] The disaster of 1898 produced two opposite movements, according to Altamira: one that was pessimistic and tried to prove that Spaniards were lacking in the essentials necessary for adapting themselves to modern civilization: the other that reacted against the pessimistic view and turned with confidence to the task of introducing a progressive spirit into the country. Madariaga in his memorable book on Spain gives a striking description of Spain on the eve of the first World War. 'One afternoon in the month of March 1914, a youthful man with a heavy forehead, expressive eyes and an attractive, if self-conscious smile, came forward on the stage of the theatre of La Comedia in Madrid and began to speak with quiet assurance, elegant gesture and a finely modulated voice to a crowded house which listened eagerly, and now and then interrupted with vigorous ovations. He was the already famous professor of metaphysics of the University of Madrid, José Ortega y Gasset. But what he was explaining to this packed theatre was no metaphysical question; it was the grief of his generation at the sight of what their elders had done with Spain. "Our generation," he said, "has never negotiated with the topics of patriotism, and

[1] R. Altamira, *op. cit.*, 2nd ed., p. 11.

when it hears the word Spain it does not think of Calderón and
Lepanto, it does not remember the victories of the Cross, it does
not call forth the vision of a blue sky, and under it a splendour—
it merely feels, and what it feels is grief." He poured scorn on what
he called "official Spain". "Official Spain" consists, as it were, in
ghostly parties upholding ghosts of ideas, which, backed by the
shadows of newspapers, keep going Cabinets of hallucination.
"The old Spain, with its governing and its governed classes is now
dying," he cried. It was high time that everything in Spain was
nationalized and liberalized. This memorable day,' adds
Madariaga, 'was the beginning of a movement of real leadership
in Spanish politics. The spring tapped by Don Francisco Giner
and fed by the devoted efforts of the *Junta* or Committee for the
development of Studies, had by now become a strong and clear
river of intelligent opinion flowing into the troubled and muddy
waters of Spanish politics.' Alas, four months after that memorable day 'an Austrian prince was killed in Sarajevo, and Europe
went mad.'[1]

In the last fifty years of troubled Spanish history some of the
most striking utterances by Spanish thinkers have been in the
form of an essay. The *ensayo* or essay has been the most popular
literary form because it embodies in concise form the dominant
ideas of the moment. Sometimes it may be a *cri du cœur* or passionate appeal by a prophet to his people. Modern Spanish
history has had many of these dramatic essays which in their
day summed up the thoughts that seethed in the minds of the
thinking minority. Before Ganivet committed suicide in the year
of Spain's disaster of 1898 he poured out his soul in one of those
essays—The *'Idearium Español'* (1897)[2]—following the motto he
had adapted from Saint Augustine: *'Noli foras ire: in interiore
Hispaniae habitat veritas.'* Altamira's work, which we have considered, is in the nature of an essay written at white heat during the
tragic war and re-edited and re-issued in 1917 during the first
Great War. Unamuno, the great master of the dramatic essay,
has used it as a means of expressing his own philosophy, and his
Quixotic self-communings. His critics tried to lay him low by calling him 'paradoxical', but paradoxes are necessary as weapons

[1] S. de Madariaga, *Spain*, revised edition, London, 1942, pp. 230–231.
[2] It has been very well translated into English by Rafael Nadal, London, 1947.

against routine of thought, and Unamuno's function in modern Spain has been to make men probe and sift ideas. 'My principal duty', he said once, 'is to irritate people. We must sow in men seeds of doubt, of distrust, of disquiet, and even of despair.' Indeed, if Unamuno had lived at Athens he would not have lasted as long as Socrates: he would have been made drink the hemlock on the plea that such a man was a danger to the state. Nevertheless, the essays of Unamuno are among the most significant pronouncements of the time. After Unamuno we come to Ortega y Gasset, who after his brilliant entry upon the stage on the eve of the first Great War published a series of essays which show most unmistakably the very essence of Spain's condition. First of all 'España Invertebrada' condenses in short space the philosophical history of Spanish political life. In spite of all his study of Kant and Hegel, Ortega remains for ever a man of the Mediterranean. Following the example of Plato, he illustrates his ideas by beautiful metaphors and images. His works never cease to be literature, and Gómez de Baquero called him the philosopher poet. Ortega in his essay dispassionately sets Spain in its place among the Latin nations and compares its development with that of the others. In Spain there has been nearly always a disproportion between the common people and the select minority. All that has been done is due to the people, and what the people have not been able to do, remained undone. While the history of France or England is one that has chiefly been created by minorities, the history of Spain has entirely been made by the masses. The cause of all Spain's misfortunes, according to Ortega, was the absence of strong Feudalism as in the case of France and England. The Visigoths, when they invaded Spain, had already become devitalized owing to their long contact with the Roman Empire and they no longer possessed the strong select minority that would have given vigour to Spain. Hence the Visigoths were unable to withstand the flood of Moslem invasion. The lack of the select minority made itself felt all through the Middle Ages, and the rapid unification in the fifteenth century, which made Spain into the first complete nation in Europe, was due to the lack of vital feudal elements within the country. Ortega contrasts the Spanish colonization of America with the English. Whereas the English colonization overseas was carried out by select groups who established in the countries beyond the seas their own social structure based upon the mother country, the Spanish colonization of America was carried out by the masses blindly and unconsciously. 'Our masses,' says Ortega, 'did all that was to be done: they populated, cultivated, sang, groaned and loved, but they could not give to the nations they created what they themselves did not possess; namely superior discipline, culture and progressive civilization.'[1]

The absence of the select minorities, he says, has influenced all Spanish history and prevented the country from reaching the normality of the other nations which sprang from similar stock. The absence of 'the best' has caused a blindness among the masses of the people which prevents them from distinguishing the good man from the bad, with the result that when privileged individuals do appear in Spain the masses are unable to recognize their merit, and frequently annihilate them. The periods of decadence in a country, according to Ortega, are those when the minority ruling the people—namely the aristocracy—has lost the sterling qualities which once raised it to its dominant position. Then the masses with justice rise in revolt against this corrupt and effete aristocracy, but instead of substituting in its place another and more virtuous aristocracy they generally eliminate all aristocratic impulses in the belief that society can exist without the qualities of the minority.[2] There is, continues Ortega, in the history of humanity a perpetual alternation of two contrasting periods: the period of growth when aristocracies and societies are formed; and the period of decadence when these aristocracies decline and the societies break up. The Indians called these periods by the names *Kitra* and *Kali* and one follows the other rhythmically. During the *Kali* period the régime of the castes degenerates, and the *Sudra*, that is to say, the inferior castes, dominate, because Brahma has fallen asleep. Then Vishnu assumes the terrible form of Siva and destroys the living and the twilight of the gods glows on the horizon. Finally, Brahma awakes: Vishnu as the kindly god appears, recreates the Cosmos afresh and introduces a new *Kitra* period.

Ortega y Gasset's celebrated essay '*España Invertebrada*'

---

[1] J. Ortega y Gasset, *España Invertebrada*, Madrid, 1925, pp. 164–165.
[2] *Ibid.*, pp. 117–118.

appeared in 1921 when Europe was struggling to recover from the first World War and when, as Madariaga said, the whole Iberian Peninsula was being rapidly over-run with Bolshevik measles which had begun in Barcelona and spread to agricultural Andalusia.[1] Hence the pessimistic tone of the essay and the emphasis laid upon mob rule of the *Kali* period. In 1930 a further prophetic essay came from the pen of Ortega y Gasset, this time one which revealed the whole trend of European affairs. The essay, which bears the resounding title, 'The Revolt of the Masses', completes the doctrine sketched out in 'Invertebrate Spain'. For many years past the prophets had announced the revolt. 'The masses are advancing,' Hegel had said apocalyptically; 'without a new spiritual power to act as guide, our epoch which is a revolutionary one will produce a catastrophe,' were the fateful words of Auguste Comte. From a rock in the Engadine Nietzsche cried: 'I see the high tide of nihilism rising.' Ortega sums up his essay as follows: 'Owing to the perfect organization given by the nineteenth century to life in certain respects, the masses, who have profited thereby, no longer remember that these benefits were the result of planning and organization, but believe they are the products of Nature herself. Hence the absurd state of mind revealed by these masses whose only thought is for their personal comfort. They forget that the benefits of civilization are due to the amazing ingenuity of the inventors and may only be maintained at the cost of constant care and effort, and they believe that all they have to do is to shout for those benefits peremptorily as though they were their natural and inalienable rights. . . .'

In conclusion, Ortega writes: 'Only the determination to construct a great nation from the group of peoples of the Continent would give new life to the pulses of Europe. . . . In my opinion the building up of Europe into a great national State is the one enterprise that could counter-balance a victory of the "Five Years Plan". Communism is an extravagant moral code, but it is nothing less than a moral code. Does it not seem more worthy and more fruitful to oppose to that Slavonic Code a new European Code, the inspiration towards a new programme of life?'

[1] S. de Madariaga, *Spain*, p. 243.

It is strange to realize that this essay which contains such amazingly prophetic words on Europe's condition should have been written in 1930 on the eve of the fall of the Spanish monarchy by one of the three intellectual leaders who founded the 'Group in the Service of the Republic' to prepare the way for the arrival of 'La Niña Bonita', 'The Pretty Girl', as the republic was quaintly called by the conspirators in the nineteenth century.[1]

There is poignant significance in Menéndez Pidal's essay on 'The Spaniards in Their History' when we reflect that it was written sixteen years after the Cassandra-like prophecies of Ortega y Gasset. Those prophecies were tragically fulfilled in the stormy years of the Republic who, though she had entered as gently as a lamb amidst the blessings of the intellectuals, yet within a year began to wear a 'bitter profile'. Menéndez Pidal, however, made the *Centro de Estudios Históricos* into a meeting-place not only of Spanish humanists but a clearing-house of European ideas of scholarship. He and his followers worked patiently at their texts, withdrawing as far as possible into their ivory tower, but theirs was a pathetic Urbino, standing like a lonely beacon on a rock buffeted on all sides by the angry waves of revolution. When we look back to those years of the Republic they stand out in one's imagination as successive scenes in a ghastly drama moving inexorably towards final doom. It was a period of frantic planning and febrile scheming; for the idealists among the intellectuals imagined they could overthrow the existing order and create a new progressive Spain without leaving a vestige of the old. But all these schemes straightway crumbled owing to the forces of revolution. The whole country was in the throes of a monstrous witches' Sabbath conjured up by a host of foreign agents eager to lead the dance. The tunes and rhythms these minions of the moon played up hill and down dale throughout the country were Spanish, but so deformed and twisted by the malignant ingenuity of these minstrels of chaos that it seemed as though the spirit of Spain had been obliterated. But through the mocking cacophony I could hear the solemn booming of the *Dies Irae* announcing the approaching doom.

Menéndez Pidal's essay must be read in the light of the grim and tragic years of the Civil War. It is not a pessimistic essay

[1] S. de Madariaga, *Spain*. pp. 292–293.

written in a moment of national disaster like that of Altamira, nor is it one written in a mood of prophecy, like that of Ortega: it is a calm dispassionate analysis of Spain's national characteristics written by a scientist and a humanist in a mood of detached inquiry. It is a concise summing up by one who has followed all the parabola of his country's history and has succeeded in outliving all prophecies. Now and then the calm surface of his style becomes ruffled with emotion and we expect that he will turn aside from his stern historical course and go off in pursuit of one of his hobbies, but he resists all such temptations and follows the path traced out from the outset. What gives the essay particular significance is that the author takes in the whole panorama of Spanish history and shows how modern tendencies are due to causes that lie embedded in the original Spanish character. Other peoples in Europe—the Italians, for instance—possess the virtue of moderation or soberness no less than the Spaniards, but the latter possess it to such a degree that it has affected their whole history and even as far back as Roman times they were credited with this virtue which is in accordance with the doctrine of Seneca, the Spanish philosopher *par excellence*. The Spaniard with his doctrine of *sustine et abstine* remains even to-day an inveterate Senecan, and this stoicism we find in the humble reaper on the parched uplands of Castile, who endures the fierce heat of the summer months without any refreshment but the lukewarm water from his earthern jar. Menéndez Pidal then shows how the physical soberness and abstemiousness of the Spaniard appears in the scant attention he gives to material interests and he quotes the famous instance of the Spanish soldiers, who, at the moment of going into battle at Pavia, gave up their pay and even handed over their personal belongings to Pescara in order to satisfy the demands of the auxiliary German troops. This detachment may even become a great defect of the Spaniard leading to his notorious indifference on occasions to the mismanagement of the vital affairs of his country. With infinite subtlety, Menéndez Pidal analyses the fundamental traits of the Spanish character and shows how certain characteristics may at times be a virtuous impulse of the individual, but on other occasions may be due to a lack of incentive. When discussing the regionalist spirit of Spain the author takes up the cudgels against foreign historians like Hume who have exaggerated the local particularism of the people, for he maintains that the dissimilarity of races in the Peninsula is not perceptibly greater than that existing, for instance, in France. The greater localism of Spain is due to the original exclusive character of the Iberians, already noted by the authors of antiquity long before there came to the Peninsula even half the number of races enumerated by Hume as causing the dispersive tendencies. In another place the author breaks a lance with Ortega y Gasset, who, in his essay, had referred to the lack of educated minorities in Spain. The Spanish people, Pidal says, have not necessarily lacked leading minorities, but those minorities have peculiar characteristics of their own which cause their actions to appear ineffective, even null and void. Spanish aristocracy, both that of talents and that of social position, has never aspired to the position of a class apart, but devotes its activities to the majority and adopts a style of unaffected simplicity based on broad human values. He also quotes Alfieri, who travelled through Spain in 1771, as stating that the Spanish and Portuguese peoples were the only ones in Europe who preserved their customs intact, and possessed the raw material for carrying out great enterprises.

When treating the problem of nationalism, Menéndez Pidal has hard words to say of the Catalan historians who have been at great pains to show that the Catalan people, through the course of centuries, had always been completely and permanently separated from the rest of the Spanish peoples. History, he says, has thus to be de-Castilianized and therefore the wrongs done to Catalonia do not spring from Philip IV or Philip V, but go back to the Middle Ages, even to Count Raymond Berenguer IV, who, they say, betrayed the Catalan cause by not taking the title of King of Catalonia and Aragon. 'Raymond Berenguer,' says the author ironically, 'ignorant of the fact that he would displease the nationalists of the twentieth century, went even further than refusing to call himself King; he actually acknowledged himself to be a vassal of the Emperor of Toledo, Alfonso VII.'

The most striking pages in the essay are devoted to the Two Spains, and here the author has embodied the essence of his humanistic philosophy. These pages sum up the thoughts that for years have continually arisen in the minds of Spanish thinkers. They are all the more significant to-day coming from the foremost scholar of the Spanish World, from one who has seen in the past so many of his ideals shattered and who yet possesses an undiminished faith in Spain's future. These pages, too, will be a revelation to those in Europe and across the seas who have shut their eyes to Spain's historical claims from the past and allowed her to be the victim, the scapegoat of world politics. Menéndez Pidal, faithful to his scientific method of investigation, studies the problem of the Two Spains back in its origins but he brings it up to the present, and the words he writes of Spain might be applied to most of the other countries of Europe, for not one is free from the dangers he enumerates: 'Larra lamented over half Spain as dead, yet the deceased rose from the tomb to continue the mortal struggle. A hundred years later, when Azaña proclaimed the death of Catholic Spain, the latter rose and it was republican Spain which fell. . . . This was the fated destiny of the two sons of Oedipus, who would not consent to reign together, and mortally wounded each other. Will this sinister craving to destroy the adversary ever cease? Evil days indeed have come before the world when extremism of a kind that leaves that of Spain far behind appears on all sides and when a ferocious cleavage such as never before existed, makes national life in common impossible in many countries owing to the exclusive tendencies which have gripped the dominant parties in the States. Mussolini called the twentieth century the era of collectivity, the century of the State; but for Italy and Germany this century lasted only a couple of decades, and although we do not yet know how the democracies will forge their victory which they share with Communism, nevertheless the individual will again win back his rights, which allow him to disagree, to rectify and invent afresh, for it is to the individual that we owe all the great deeds of history.'

And let us take leave of Menéndez Pidal the scholar, the humanist, the minstrel ballad-chaser and the patriot, cherishing in our memories his passionate appeal for the eternal single Spain that exists deep down in the soul of every Spaniard: it is not one of the half Spains facing the other that will survive as a single party with the epitaph of the other part; it will be the complete Spain for whom so many have longed, the Spain that has not amputated one of her limbs, but makes full use of all her capabilities for honest toil in order to win a place among the peoples that give the impulse to modern life.

Walter Starkie

THE SPANIARDS IN
THEIR HISTORY
by Ramón Menéndez Pidal

The Spaniards in
their History[1]

The facts of history do not repeat themselves, but Man the Maker of History is always the same. Hence the eternally true saying: *Quid est quod fuit? Ipsum quod futurum est*—What happened in the past? What will happen in the future. Consequently, mankind has always been eager to know how, given its permanent identity, each people has behaved in history. Even in the days when our mediaeval historiography was in its infancy writers often considered it necessary to add to the narration of events a description of the various peoples according to their dominant quality. For instance we find attached to the *Epítome Ovetense*[2] of 883 a chapter entitled *De proprietatibus gentium*, which signalizes the Greeks by their wisdom, the Goths by their valour, the Franks by their fierceness, the Gauls by their trading. Other chronicles point out the salient vices and virtues of each human group; the deceitfulness and wisdom of the Greeks, the violence as well as the acuteness of the Spaniards (this observation is not far from the truth), the fierceness as well as the steadfastness of the Franks. These definite characteristics of different peoples with which to a greater or lesser degree writers have concerned themselves from the earliest times, should be extensively treated in any History, but on this occasion I shall limit myself to defining certain Spanish characteristics which I consider to be the basis of the rest, and I shall attempt to give a general survey of those tendencies which have most constantly operated through every period, whether favourably or unfavourably. In this way we shall be able to understand the peaks and depressions of Spain's historical curve.

I shall keep two objectives before me; first I wish to show that every quality is, as it were, two-faced; it may cause positive or

---

[1] The footnotes to this essay have been supplied by the translator unless otherwise noted.

[2] This history, dating from the reign of Alfonso III in Oviedo, was the first to be written by the Christians of the north of Spain after the Moslem invasion.

negative results according to the direction it takes or the circumstances in which it is developed; secondly that even the most permanent characteristics do not necessarily operate, for although they may appear in the majority of a people they do not always determine its actions, and they may even in certain circumstances be limited to a minority. Furthermore, although those characteristics survive through the centuries this does not mean that they are unchangeable. We are not dealing with any somatic or racial determinism but with historical aptitudes and habits which can, and will, vary according to the occupations and interests of life, the type of education, social relationships, and other circumstances.

Chapter I

Material and Moral Austerity

Many writers have pointed out the close connection between the character of the Spaniards and the land they inhabit. Unamuno is insistent on this point. He holds that the harsh, dry spirit of our people with its lack of the sense of compromise is intimately connected with the landscape of the central meseta, which is hard in outline, devoid of trees, boundless in horizon. The light there dazzles, the climate reaches extremes, and there are no gentler aspects of nature. But this correspondence does not apply to the climates that exist outside the two Castiles. The same physical austerity may also be found in the smiling, fertile Andalusia, and in my opinion, austerity is the basic quality of the Spanish character; it does not depend upon any Castilian geographical determinism, but is so universal that if we start from it we shall be able to understand the remaining characteristics we must now define.

The most penetrating description of the Spanish character given in ancient times was by the Gaul Trogus Pompeius.[1] He begins by saying that the Spaniard has a body adapted for abstinence and toil, for hard and rigid sobriety in all things, *dura omnibus et adstricta parsimonia*. From Trogus onward we find many references to austere simplicity, even to a glaring heedlessness of comforts prevalent in certain aspects of life in Spain. We may recall that, during the centuries when all the precious metals of the New World were flowing into the Peninsula, foreigners found our houses more modestly furnished than the

[1] Roman historian of the first century, of Gallic nationality, author of a Universal History (*Historiae Philippicae*) which has been lost, but of which there remains an Epitome written in the second century by Justin. The last book, No. 44, deals with Spain.

French, the meals very meagre, our University halls lacking in comforts (the students had to prop their notebooks on their knees); our inns very inhospitable; the public services of Madrid very inadequate, a fact that worried Philip II; in short, a way of life devoid of comfort. That is to say that all the wealth amassed by the American colonists and carried back annually in the fleets of the State was not applied by the Spaniards to the comfort and well-being of their private life or to the embellishment of their cities. Even to-day the Spaniard contents himself with little, and we continually see around us examples of that austerity allied to hard work to which Trogus referred. The humblest of all is the reaper in our fields—an astonishing specimen of *dura et adstricta parsimonia*. During the most oppressive heat of summer, without any refreshment but the lukewarm water of his earthern jar, poorly clad and poorly fed, he seems to possess nothing in the world but stoical contentment in his work.

This neglect of material necessities to which we have referred agrees with Seneca's doctrine that he who has but little is not poor, but poor is he who covets more, for the natural necessities of life are very few while those of vain ambition are inexhaustible. The Spaniard, inured to privations, believes in the doctrine of *sustine et abstine*, 'bear and forbear', and this rule of conduct sets man above all adversity. In his character there is an element of instinctive stoicism; he is a born disciple of Seneca. For this reason Spanish philosophical thinkers through the centuries have always turned to Seneca as their favourite author. A great debt certainly is owed to him, but Seneca himself, the refiner of stoicism, owed a great deal to the fact that he sprang from a Spanish family.

Due to this instinctive influence of Seneca the Spaniard can as readily endure privations as he can withstand the disturbing temptations to greed and self-indulgence, for his innate soberness inclines him towards a certain ethical austerity. This shows itself in the general tenor of his life, with its simplicity, dignity even in the humblest classes, and strong family ties. The Spanish people preserve these deep natural qualities unimpaired as a kind of human reserve, whereas other races which are more tainted by the luxuries of civilization find themselves constantly threatened by a process of wear and tear which saps their strength. It is of interest to point out some aspects of this vital austerity as an illustration of historical characteristics. We shall pay special attention to the observations made by foreign writers because they are always better qualified to note what is peculiar to a country, even though we should discount the element of superficiality that is so often to be found in travellers' impressions.

DETACHMENT

The connection between physical soberness and other qualities is clearly shown by the scant attention Spaniards give to material interests, for owing to their hermit-like abstemiousness they find the strength to resist the pressure of material necessities. To this are due the not infrequent cases of collective generosity noted by historians. The Spanish soldier is a special case in point: even though he may mutiny like any other when his pay is lacking, yet he can always rise above himself when the situation demands it. At the moment of going into battle at Pavia the Spaniards gave up their pay and even handed over their personal belongings to Pescara in order to satisfy the demands of the German auxiliaries. Another example is given by Calderón in the 'Sitio de Breda'[1] Act III, Scene 2, when the Spaniards offer their gains to the foreign troops on condition that the latter refrain from sacking the city, for thus the victory would be the nobler. Each one of those soldiers might appear as the hero in a tale of disinterested generosity. That so many together should have acted in this way is an exception to the rule that generous gestures are isolated occurrences standing out in antithesis to the collective self-interest of the mass.

It is also a natural trait in the Spaniard not to allow any calculation of gains and losses to prevail over considerations of another order. Columbus, a foreigner by birth, instead of allowing himself to be carried away by enthusiasm for his enterprise, kept postponing it while he negotiated interminably, and refused to risk the venture until he had secured for himself a dazzling series of profits and rewards. Whereas a host of Spanish explorers, despising material advantage, engaged in perilous exploits for the

[1] Calderón's comedy refers to the Dutch stronghold of Breda, captured by the Spaniards under the command of the Marquis of Spinola in 1626, after ten months' siege.

simple love of adventure, or with only problematic hopes of gain.

This characteristic may be observed in many aspects of private or public life, for it has always been a great quality as well as a great defect of the Spaniard to allow himself to be swayed by idealistic motives rather than by the desire for economic profit. The reduction of necessities may at one moment be a virtuous impulse in the individual, inspiring generous action, but on other occasions it may be due to a lack of incentive which produces aversion to work. This may explain both the collective abnegation displayed by the Spanish people in various circumstances, and during whole epochs of their history, as well as their notorious indifference to the mismanagement of the vital affairs of their country.

Those who, over a long period, have noted how industrial and commercial interests in Spain have been neglected explain it in various ways. In the time of the Catholic King, in 1513, Guicciardini[1] attributes it to the fact that the artisans had a *fumo di fidalgo*—pretensions to nobility—and preferred to dedicate themselves to war; a similar explanation to that given by Saavedra Fajardo[2] who referred to the 'haughty and exalted' spirit of the nation, shown even among the plebeian classes by their contempt for any occupation that was unworthy of one who was noble. At other times when the warrior spirit did not prevail, Ferdinand de la Torre,[3] describing to Henry IV in 1455 a dispute he had held with a certain Frenchman before the King of France, stated that in his opinion foreigners were more industrious and wealthy than Spaniards, because their lands were less fertile than Spain; an explanation which was repeated by the Ambassador of the Sultan of Morocco at the court of Charles II in 1690. No doubt he had heard it from Spaniards who quoted the mediaeval 'Eulogies' of Spain. This so-called abundance of Spain might in the sixteenth and seventeenth centuries have been confused with the abundance of silver and gold that arrived from America. But

[1] The Florentine historian and politician Francesco Guicciardini, 1483–1540, ambassador at the court of Ferdinand the Catholic, 1512–1513, was the author of *Diario del viaggio in Spagna*.

[2] Diego Saavedra Fajardo, 1584–1648, writer and diplomat. His *Empresas políticas o Idea de un príncipe cristiano*, 1640, is frequently quoted in the present work.

[3] Fernando de la Torre, poet and prose writer of the middle of the fifteenth century, was a native of Burgos and studied in Florence. (He was at the court of Charles VII of France, 1422–1461.)

these examples merely illustrate the essential truth that a Spaniard will always sacrifice his desire for wealth or comfort to idealistic motives of pride or glory no matter how vain they may be.

The observations given by travellers from the seventeenth to the nineteenth centuries agree with this judgment. One who visited the court of Philip III at Valladolid noted that the handicraftsmen worked disdainfully, as though merely to get out of a difficulty, and he saw some, especially the silversmiths, seated at work with their cloaks on. As soon as they had collected 200 or 300 reals they girded on their swords and strutted about like noblemen until they had spent the money, when they would return to their work. Such was the impression of another traveller who visited the Spain of Isabel II: he did not describe the Andalusian workman as lazy, but noted that as soon as he had gathered a handful of reals, he would throw his embroidered jacket over his shoulder, pick up his guitar and go off to sport among his friends or pay court to the girls, until lack of money would force him to return to work. This interruption of work was not a daily occurrence and was not caused by exhaustion necessitating long periods of rest for rebuilding energy, but by a weakening of the stimulus to work. Once his urgent material necessities had been satisfied, his attention would wander off after other incentives which appeared more attractive. The Spaniard possesses the invaluable treasure of soberness which delivers him from many embarrassing cares, but as a rule he does not make the best use of that precious quality when troubles and anxieties have really to be faced. Nevertheless this disinclination to work which has been so often noted through the centuries has, on frequent occasions, been remedied. Guicciardini himself related how a revival of industry took place under the Catholic Monarchs, and he described the looms of Valencia, Toledo, and Seville with their luxurious woven stuffs of crimson and gold, and this was confirmed by Navagero in 1526. Noteworthy, too, was the great impulse given to industry all through Spain by the efforts of Ferdinand VI and Charles III which were so successful that they roused the jealousy of the more commercial countries, as was admitted by W. Robertson in 1777. Gracián points to a special aspect of this indifference when discussing the Spanish tendency to abandon tasks already begun. Paying a tribute to the constancy in work of foreign countries, he writes: 'Impatience—that is the defect of the Spaniards, just as Patience is the virtue of the Belgians; the latter complete what they have begun, whereas the Spaniards leave the task unfinished; they toil and moil until they have mastered the difficulties, then they stop, for they do not know how to follow up their victories.' The physical and mental soberness of the Spaniard causes him to remain satisfied with immediate results; consequently he is not interested in anything that can be achieved only slowly and at a later date. He dislikes having to pursue further what has already been attained, for this would, in his opinion, be to confess his lack of the essential soberness. Hence he despises the quality of patience so eulogized by Gracián, calling it unreasonable obstinacy, the failing of those who are as slow in wits as they are in action.

Furthermore, owing to his arrogant or lazy self-confidence, he gives no heed to the morrow: sufficient for the day is the evil thereof; there is no need to fret about what to-morrow will bring. The most striking examples of this lack of foresight were those which occurred at a time when Spain's activity was at its zenith, and though this did not prevent her triumph it seriously hampered it. It is significant to note that in so important a question as finance, at the most critical moment of the supreme struggle of the Counter-Reformation, Philip II was able to solve his economic difficulties only at the cost of increasing his huge debts to the Genoese. This was because he never made allocations from one year to the next to meet the extraordinary expenditure which continually was necessary, but lived for the day, meeting each difficulty when it presented itself, as the Venetian Ambassador noted in 1573, among other examples of damaging lack of foresight.

Later on Spanish writers express surprise that the fifteen or sixteen millions in gold and silver which came annually from the Indies were sufficient to flood Europe as far as Constantinople with Castilian money, yet were not enough to prevent all the bills of exchange from ending up in the hands of the Genoese bankers. These latter could not be dispensed with because of the scant attention paid by the Spaniards to banking, owing to the defect of 'impatience' we have discussed above, in this instance alleged by Suárez de Figueroa.

Another instance often mentioned by Spanish critics is that which gives origin to the proverbial phrase explained by Tirso in '*El Celoso Prudente*': 'You are succour from Spain, useless because too late.' Cervantes in his play '*El Gallardo Español*' makes the King of Algiers assert confidently that the help the Spaniards intend to bring to Oran will arrive too late. This same conviction is the cause of the bitterness Quevedo felt in his last days (May–June 1645), when he wondered anxiously whether help would be brought in time to Rosas (town in Catalonia), for he felt that its fall was inevitable if it did not receive the necessary aid. Correas in his '*Vocabulario*' tries to diminish the reproach contained in the well-known phrase when he says: '*Socorros de España*; a complaint at the tardy arrival of help, an ordinary occurrence in great Empires; the same was said of Athens in her day.' But the proverbial phrase with its reproach was current before Spain had any extensive Empire, namely in the first half of the fifteenth century at least, for Díez de Gámez in his '*Victorial*' alludes to it when he compares the psychology of the three nations thus: 'The English remember before the event; they are prudent. The French never remember until the event is upon them; they are proud and hasty. The Castilians never remember until the event has passed; they are lazy and contemplative.' Contemplative, yes, in their bad moments, when they turn aside from action and go in quest of some vain fantasy, like the sluggish nobleman of Pérez de Ayala,[1] who renounces all enterprise as vain and futile, for

'over his head lingers the butterfly of dreams and the scorpion of laziness'.

Improvidence is double-faced; beside the contemplative kind mentioned by Díez de Gámez is the active improvidence which far from delaying action drives men into it, throwing all caution to the winds. The audacious exploration of the Amazon was carried out without the slightest preparation, and it would never have been accomplished if the explorers had insisted beforehand upon a plan guaranteeing the success of the enterprise. Indeed a great part of the American colonization and the history of Spain itself is a series of hazardous improvisations. The same may be said of the other aspects of detachment and improvidence which

[1] Ramón Pérez de Ayala, modern novelist, in *La Caída de los Limones*, 1920.

have likewise their positive side. At the very moment when Philip II's finances had failed repeatedly through lack of provident care, the same characteristically Spanish detachment drove Castile to engage in the noblest action in our history and sacrifice to the duties of imperial hegemony all her own comforts and advantages. Fernández Navarrete[1] in 1619 made pertinent references to the unusual method of governing always employed by Castile, adding that 'whereas Castile being the head ought to be the most privileged in the matter of payment of taxes and tributes yet it is she who contributes most for the defence and protection of the rest of the Kingdom. Not only does she contribute to the upkeep of the Royal House and the protection of the entire coast of Spain, but also to the garrisons in Italy, the forces in Africa, the subduing of Flanders and even to the succouring of foreign provinces and princes.' This conscientious self-denial in imperial matters wins a somewhat grudging tribute from a certain French traveller in 1612, who describes how the Castilians bore the chief burdens of war and government owing to their obedient subservience to their superiors, and their talent for command. He adds: 'It is extraordinary how being so few, they can yet win such renown in the wars in Europe. They are like the Macedonians in Greece, long-suffering, hard as well as ambitious, cruel, greedy and ostentatious: they are all-powerful in Europe and the Indies.'

APATHY AND ENERGY

A general indifference towards prosperity or adversity brings calmness to the mind, that imperturbable tranquillity so characteristic of Spain in the Golden Age. This quality, though it does not reach the extremes of stoical *apathia* is related to it as also is the doctrine of *nada te turbe* ('let nothing perturb thee') sublimated by our mystics: that Spanish calmness, 'that beautiful virtue of Castile' mentioned by Filippo Sassetti and noted by Renaissance Italy with admiration not unmixed with irony in the haughty viceroy of Naples as well as in the most wretched Spaniard, for ever penniless, but never without his serenity. This

[1] Pedro Fernández Navarrete, canon of Santiago Cathedral, was the author of *Conservación de Monarquías, discursos políticos dirigidos a Felipe III*, 1619; a book frequently reprinted until the nineteenth century.

quality left its mark on the Italian character and is reflected in the Hispanic word *sussiego* which denotes that virtue of a tranquil mind, and grave serenity.

This tranquillity of spirit was the virtue so praised in Charles V, for he was as unassuming in the hour of triumph as he was undismayed in adversity. His only gesture at Madrid when he learnt the great news of the battle of Pavia was to retire to his oratory to give thanks to God for having thus manifested His justice, but as the victory was at the cost of Christian blood he allowed no rejoicings at court. He was worthy to rule as Emperor and give impulse to the serene efficiency of the Spaniards who were eager to complete the greatness of their sixteenth century.

But this imperturbable serenity has its double aspect, for as well as calm serenity at the moment of energetic action, there is the calmness of apathy. In that phlegmatic Madrid society created by Philip II's ministers, who were nicknamed 'Ministers of Eternity', a young German baron wrote despairingly in 1599 of the slowness and delays of the Spanish officials in negotiating, for this slowness made him lose days and days, and similar comment was made by another *Monsieur sans-délai*, victim of the 'Come back to-morrow' system described by Larra[1] in 1833, and as common a feature to-day as in the past.

Then when decadence had become a reality, when misfortunes multiplied, another state of mind grew up related to this calmness—the Spanish 'doesn't matter', 'what's it matter?' This attitude, too, has a double facet, for it is a cross between the indifferent and the devil-may-care. Francisco Santos[2] in his book '*El No Importa de España*', written during years of national disaster (1668), described only the negative aspects. He witnesses everywhere Spaniards adopting the devil-may-care attitude to justify their own faults. Out of flattery he finds praiseworthy the indifference of Philip IV, but even then it is to show that when the king receives news of some disaster his only reaction is to order the celebration of the Forty Hours in the royal chapel. He is the lazy, apathetic king very much in tune with the rest of the easy going Spaniards listed by Francisco Santos. Santos did not live

[1] Mariano José de Larra (1809–1837), author of plays, novels and many newspaper articles dealing with customs, political and literary criticism.
[2] The author of many books, especially dealing with customs, such as *Día y Noche de Madrid*, 1663, *El No Importa de España*, 1668, etc.

on into the more hopeful times when he might have noticed that when a Spaniard feels the urge to engage in an enterprise which he considers of great moment, his very devil-may-care attitude enables him to recover unimpaired all his energies, with the result that even the severest reverses will not dishearten him.

Spaniards are always torn between two extremes: when they are eager to reach a decision they display inexhaustible vigour, but they show scant interest in the activities of everyday. They can endure the greatest hardship in any perilous and protracted expedition, but they are unable to withstand the monotony of daily toil. On the one hand they are high-spirited; that is their devil-may-care attitude: on the other hand they are dispirited, when their attitude is 'I don't give a damn'. Strong to face the worst, slack to procure the best, if in some respects theirs is the *apathia* of the stoics, in others it is mere commonplace apathy.

In its stoical aspect the apathy of Spaniards does not mean that they are merely impassive: rather does it mean acceptance of destiny which may even produce in them an attitude towards life of satisfaction and contentment. An English traveller who visited the Peninsula in 1830 wrote as follows: 'The happiness displayed by the people of all classes in spite of their misfortunes, privations, and grinding poverty is scarcely believable. Not a complaint comes from any of them, and they possess an innate dignity which prevents them from lamenting their fate even in private, and perhaps in this alone are they reserved.' Similar tributes are repeated by other foreign observers, and at this point we again recall Seneca, who held that contented poverty was not poverty, and there is no doubt that this sentiment predominates to a striking degree in the Spanish people.

The imperturbable, contented, 'what's it matter?' attitude united to soberness has created a belief in the mind of the Spaniards that they are able to endure greater hardships than other peoples and that this quality enables them to perform deeds that would be impossible to others. In the eleventh century the '*Historia Silense*'[1] states that the long-drawn-out war against the advancing force of the Saracens could only be waged by the hardened Knights of Spain, not by the self-indulgent peers of

[1] The so-called *Historia Silense* is a history of Spain written about 1118, probably in León, by an anonymous monk.

Charlemagne who retired from Saragossa longing to refresh themselves in the baths of Aachen. And in the thirteenth century Archbishop Roderick of Toledo[1] relates proudly though sadly that the crusaders from beyond the mountains, disgusted by a temporary scarcity of provisions which was soon after remedied, returned to their country, leaving the Spaniards to wage alone the gigantic battle of *Navas de Tolosa*. Afterwards every account of our wars or explorations describes episodes of amazing endurance against fatigue and fasting, of fearlessness in the face of death. It is this robust physical and spiritual constitution, with its inexhaustible reserves of energy, which explains the greater part of our history from the transcendental deeds performed in the unremitting war against Islam, as related by the historians mentioned above, to the countless enterprises in the old and new world at the beginning of the Modern Age. The Spaniards needed no more than the short space of fifty years to discover the lands and oceans forming an entire hemisphere of our planet; to explore, subdue and civilize immense territories, subjecting thousands of tribes and vast barbarian empires. Any other people less hardened to privations and risks would have needed five centuries, for they would have found it necessary to plan out their enterprises so as to reduce to the minimum the discomforts and the unfavourable contingencies. Two hundred years it took Rome to dominate the barbarian tribes of Spain alone.

HUMANITARIANISM AND BROTHERHOOD

Soberness is a quality that is highly equalitarian. When material it is a precious boon possessed by the humble no less than by the powerful; when mental it has no need of accidental or secondary distinctions. Thus the Spaniard is by nature inclined to stoical thought as refined by Seneca: man's only value is the soul which makes the servant equal to the master.

Owing to its innate stoicism no people is more intimately conscious of the Christian doctrine establishing the equality of all human beings in the sight of God the Creator and Redeemer, and

[1] Rodrigo Jiménez de Rada, Archbishop of Toledo, author of the most widely known history of mediaeval Spain, *De Rebus Hispaniae*, finished in 1243. He took part in the battle of *las Navas de Tolosa*, 1212, the most memorable battle in the Reconquest when a great invading army of 'Almohades' from Africa was conquered.

it is to this quality that Spain owes her historical position in the
colonization of America. Columbus suggested to the Catholic
Monarchs the enslavement of the Indians as though this were the
most natural proposal in the world; it was an economic proposi-
tion at so much a head. Father Las Casas,[1] though an apologist of
the discoverer, attacked him harshly for making profit out of
slaves, and at the same time recalled the words used by Queen
Isabel when she indignantly denounced the transaction: 'By what
authority does the Admiral venture thus to dispose of my vassals?' The queen always considered the Indians her vassals as she
did the Castilians, and afterwards the Catholic King invoked the
equality of all races as the fundamental principle of colonization
in the celebrated Injunction on the just dominion of Spain in the
Indies, an injunction that was drawn up for the expedition of
Pedro Arias de Avila,[2] and which began by explaining to the
Indians how God created Adam, 'from whom you and we and all
men in the world are descended'. This sense of human brotherhood was felt by every Spanish colonizer, with the consequence
that whereas the English or the Dutch did not fuse their blood
with that of the nations whom they colonized, but considered
themselves a race apart, and did not strive to attract the native
into the family of European civilization, the Spaniards, on the
other hand, from the earliest days of the discovery, pursued an
active policy of crossbreeding and at the same time devoted
themselves to giving the natives both religious and cultural
education. In the internal affairs of Spain this humanitarian
spirit shows itself in a strong tendency towards levelling social
categories and classes. He who feels great would consider his
greatness diminished if it was founded on vanity. Trogus
Pompeius notes that Viriathus, in spite of his famous deeds, and
his repeated victories over the consular armies, did not change his
former habits whether in dress, arms or food, so that any plain
soldier seemed richer than the general. Trajan was praised a

[1] Fray Bartolomé de Las Casas, native of Seville (1474–1566), Dominican,
Bishop of Chiapas in Guatemala 1544; consecrated his life to the defence of the
Indians against the abuses of the Spanish colonists. He wrote the *Historia de las
Indias* up to 1520 and a *Brevísima relación de la destrucción de las Indias*, 1552.

[2] Pedro Arias de Avila (or Pedrarias Davila), appointed governor of Tierra-
Firme (the coasts of Panama, Colombia, and Venezuela) in 1514, was ordered
to address to the Indians a *Requerimiento* in which was stated the claim of the King of
Spain to dominate and evangelize the lands recently discovered.

hundred times by Pliny for his modesty and temperate habits. Theodosius, sober in behaviour as he was in his appetite, and humble in his self-imposed penance at Thessalonica, according to Saint Augustine 'despised all human glory'. And this humble sober-mindedness continued to be the typical and unvarying quality. The greatest praise which Hernando del Pulgar[1] could give to his distinguished men, cardinals, grand masters and noblemen was to say: 'He was a genuine man, a hater of appearances,' or else: 'He was a true man and never made show of what he possessed or what he was doing.' The historians take special pains to praise in their heroes their unaffected familiarity with their subordinates and their own behaviour as true and genuine men.

Along with this simple familiarity in high born men we find in the lower classes, even in the poor, the essence of dignity and noble bearing. We all know the type of Spanish beggar who resembles a nobleman come down in the world. A Frenchman who visited Spain at the beginning of the seventeenth century was astonished to hear even a poor squire of no consequence boast of his noble stock, saying: 'I am as much a noble as the king, aye, and nobler, for he is half Flemish.' As a consequence of all this we find the same observation constantly repeated by historians; in the time of Philip IV, Saavedra Fajardo noted that the distinction between nobles and people was less marked in Spain than in Germany; in the time of Charles III, Cadalso,[2] and in the time of Isabel II Balmes,[3] both make the same observation, namely that there is no country in the world where there is more levelling of classes than in Spain. In Spain, Balmes added, a man of the humblest class in society will stop in the road the highest magnate in the land. We Spaniards, he goes on, lack the aristocratic aloofness of the English: people of high category, when we meet them,

[1] Ambassador and chronicler of the Catholic Monarchs, author of a series of twenty-four personal portraits of the fifteenth century, *Claros Varones de Castilla*, printed in Toledo 1486, and of a *Crónica de los Reyes Católicos*.

[2] José de Cadalso (1741–1782), cavalry officer killed in the siege of Gibraltar; lyric and dramatic poet and author of prose works. The work here quoted is entitled *Cartas Marruecas*, which the author pretends to have been written by a Morrocan traveller, Gazel, criticizing Spanish customs of his time. They were published posthumously in 1789.

[3] Jaime Balmes (1810–1848), Catalan priest, author of important philosophical works. The quotations are mostly from his newspaper articles of 1840–1846, collected by him and entitled *Escritos Políticos*, Madrid, 1847.

bid us drop the ceremonious form of address straightway: if they are slow in doing so, we use the familiar form without asking permission, in this way making the conversation informal. About the same time Théophile Gautier pointed out that Spain was the true home of equality where a beggar lights his cigarette butt from the cigar of a great lord, and the latter lets him do so without any trace of condescension; the marchioness steps smiling over the ragged bodies of the beggars who sleep on her threshold, and when she is on a journey she has no hesitation in drinking out of the same glass as her coachman. What a contrast with the English who used to have their letters served on a tray and pick them up with silver tongs!

Many remarkable instances of this sense of human brotherhood among the different classes in society might be quoted from Spanish history and they can be found even in remote days though we lack general descriptions of the kind here noted. Very early in the tenth century the villeins began to enter into the order of chivalry at the invitation of the Counts of Castile, Garci Fernández and Sancho García. In this democratic procedure Castile was in advance of the kingdoms of León and Aragon, as in another reform of capital importance, the abolition of serfdom.

TRADITIONALISM AND MISONEISM

To material soberness, then, corresponds moderation in aspirations and aims. Given this, the Spaniard, satisfied with what he has always possessed, does not feel the craving for new satisfactions. But this refers only to the cultural field, for in adventurous enterprises the Spaniard has always been pre-eminent. Hazardous adventures in far off lands have always made a powerful appeal to him as we may see from the picaresque novels which describe this tendency in everyday life, while the exploration of America gives us plenty of historical examples. On the other hand the Spaniard is not interested in obtaining general cultural knowledge of foreign countries, hence he is not a lover of travel for travel's sake. In cultural matters new theories instead of rousing his interest rather put him on his guard, and he is inclined to distrust them. Thus among the fundamental meanings of the Latin word *novitas*, the French take as the predominating one the positive value given to *haute nouveauté* and *nouveautés*, while the Spaniard allows the depreciatory meaning to dominate in the common phrase *sin novedad* which, when applied to any situation implies in any change that may occur a possible turn for the worse. This negative value given to the word develops in other languages too, but not to the same degree as in Spanish where the depreciatory sense suggests a note of severe warning, and this precisely in the period of greatest material activity. Guevara in the first pages of his *Marcus Aurelius* warns his readers against the many dangers that spring from novelties, and states that in his opinion it is best to set oneself against all changes. Thus admonishing the President of Granada in 1531, he said: 'Do not attempt to introduce new things, for novelties bring in their train anxieties for those who sponsor them and beget troubles among the people.' Even when giving a cold lexical definition Covarrubias feels it necessary to add a note of warning: '*Novedad*, something new and unaccustomed. It is wont to be dangerous because it means changing what has been sanctioned by ancient usage.'

For the Spaniard, therefore, it is safer to cling to what is ancient, for this is in accordance with the sober and austere style of life. But this soberness implies a negative element which bans all progress in the name of the misoneism recommended by Guevara.

A greater or less degree of traditionalism can never be an infallible touchstone for testing the genuine qualities of a people. A people may be very traditionalist and yet at the same time evolutionist, as for instance the English. A country's traditions may become deeply permeated by new progressive ideas, while innovations may imply retrogression and decline. Traditionalism should not be given all the blame for the backwardness of the Spanish people. In fact to the traditionalist spirit we owe the best that Spain has produced, the tardy fruits of its culture to which I shall refer later on. Traditionalism in itself is a positive force, the only system suited to a strong personality. Misoneism is the negative side of traditionalism, for it means the rejection of all that is new, and it has in certain periods of Spanish history hindered the nation's progress when to it is added the general apathy of the people. Where soberness of aims may be most clearly seen in relation to the dangers of misoneistic traditionalism is, to quote an example, in the field of scientific studies which continually aim at enlarging their scope progressively. Often in our writers do we meet the declaration that all sciences which do not teach man to live healthily and honestly are of no consequence, and there is no doubt that the Spaniards' indifference to pure science, which in their opinion is superfluous, is due to the innate tendencies inherited from Seneca of which we have already spoken. Seneca disapproved of philosophical and grammatical discussions that were too theoretical, for he considered that they did not help to perfect the moral nature of man or give him that wisdom which leads to the Highest Good; 'to wish to know more than is necessary is a kind of intemperance,' it is to fail in the quality of *sobrietas* or soberness: *plus scire velle quam sit satis, imtemperantiae genus est.* The same comforting thought may be derived by Spaniards from the words of Saint Paul, if applied loosely to profane science: 'Do not wish to know more than is necessary, but know with moderation,' *sapere ad sobrietatem.* This meagreness of men's aspirations was not perceptible in mediaeval periods of splendour (Arab-Spanish science; Toledan translations; Alfonso X). But from the beginning of the Modern Age the difference was very marked between Spain and the other peoples who gave impetus to knowledge. The writers of the golden centuries (without taking their authority from the doctrine of Seneca, though he was a very familiar author to them) considered it a special virtue of their own to avoid busying themselves in what they called the vain discussions of the humanists and grammarians, so popular in Europe, in order to concentrate their attention upon the 'necessary' sciences, namely theology, dialectic, law, medicine, in which, they boasted arrogantly, Spain was superior to all other nations; and they were right as regards certain branches of those sciences. Later on, when the decadence began, misoneism developed, and there was a well-known maxim which stated that to say *novedad* or novelty was the same as to say *no verdad*, no verity. Hence the aversion or at least the indifference to all progress which lay like a dead weight over the nation. Whenever it was possible to conquer this spirit of neglect we find an immediate advance in scientific work, always in bitter opposition to the reactionary tendencies.

LATE AND EARLY FRUITS

The most successful products of the Spanish genius have been created as a result of the constant effort to give life and perfection to individual qualities sprung from traditional roots, but ripened at a late season. Such fruits are esteemed for their rarity; being no longer found in other countries they introduce elements whose efficacy has been missed.

The best examples are to be discovered in the Renaissance, the period which was in other countries radically modernist, but in Spain made a truce with traditionalism, thus avoiding as far as was possible a break with the Middle Ages. This break was practically complete in other countries but Spain remained staunchly loyal to the great truths and beauties of the Middle Ages and strove to revive them, adapting them to the new spirit of the Renaissance. The Spanish Monarchy from Ferdinand the Catholic for the two ensuing centuries is conceived as a Renaissance state which still supports the mediaeval doctrine of universal Catholicism. The imperial idea of Charles V was based upon a similar combination of principles. Saint Ignatius keeping vigil in Montserrat[1] gave life to the metaphorical idea of 'spiritual knighthood' so dear to the Middle Ages, but he also gave a new meaning to asceticism in his foundation of the great religious order of modern times. Other examples were the restoration of scholastic philosophy which had such a long flowering under Vitoria, Soto, Maldonado, and Suárez and afterwards extended its vast influence over other Catholic countries; the development of contrapuntal technique on traditional foundations in the fifteenth and sixteenth centuries with masters like the Andalusian Ramos de Pareja, the Toledan Diego Ortiz, Antonio de Cabezón and Francisco de Salinas from Burgos, Tomás Luis de Vitoria from Avila, all of whom had great influence in Italy and Germany; finally mysticism, the *Romancero*, the books of chivalry, the drama, all are further examples of late ripening fruits, the slow evolution of some mediaeval type, which were very much appreciated outside Spain and exercised admitted influence. All those

---

[1] St Ignatius watched over his arms the night of the 24th to the 25th March, 1522, in front of the altar of Our Lady of Montserrat, in order to become a Knight of Christ, thus imitating the ceremony of watching the arms which used to be performed by the aspirant knight on the eve of his installation.

achievements were accomplished with a broad sweep, and continuous effort truly national in character. At a later date we have the War of Independence when Spain, in defence of her traditional institutions, made a concerted nationalist movement which was admired by all, and which was instrumental in giving back to revolutionary Europe a restorative monarchical spirit.

When we contrast the broad continuous policy on traditionalist lines backed by the majority of the nation, with the programme of innovations put forward by a minority group of reformers, we find that the latter seems unstable and unsubstantial by comparison. Even the most successful individual enterprises fail for lack of some one to carry them on, and once this happens it is necessary to start afresh from the very beginning. Owing to envy, that distinctive element of the Spanish character, which I shall discuss presently, no one is willing to attach any value to the work of others, for it seems that to give any credit to another means to curtail one's own. Thus masters do not found schools, and in consequence their teaching does not reach its possible perfection, or pave the way for higher development by later masters. This is the reason why Spain is a country of forerunners, who lead the way only to become forgotten, once their innovation reaches another country, readier to receive and develop it. Examples of these early fruits, as we might call them, which never ripen to their full may be found even in the Renaissance itself. Take the case of the Grand Master of the Order of St John, Fernández de Heredia. It was he who gave the earliest impulse to Greek scholarship by, among other remarkable works, his Aragonese translation, about 1385, of the first text of Plutarch known to the West (it was soon to be translated in its turn from Aragonese into Italian). But this precocious enthusiasm did not find any support and it remains as a pathetic isolated example. Feijóo noted various examples of forgotten precursors such as Antonio Agustín in medal-coining and Fray Pedro Ponce in the art of deaf and dumb language.

As a result of all this lack of continued effort the vital evolution of Spain, both in intellectual culture as well as in political action, has produced its moments of intensity only at long intervals; in fact it represents a curve with peak points widely spaced out, its sound waves are long and their deep low tone is less often heard than that of other great peoples. The peak points are few and far between and the sound only occasionally becomes sharper and more perceptible.

Chapter II

Idealism

BEYOND DEATH

Among the special characteristics of the Spanish peoples handed down to us by ancient authors, Livy relates that when the Iberians north of the Ebro were forced by Cato to disarm, many committed suicide, for owing to their fierce pride they held that life without arms was of no value. Strabo,[1] giving examples of ferocity, describes how, in the Cantabrian wars, mothers killed their children rather than allow them to fall into the power of their enemies. A youth, whose father and brothers were chained up as prisoners, killed them all at the father's orders. He also relates how a woman killed her fellow captives. Belonging to a civilization already in decline, Strabo sees in this only the barbarian side, but he points out other examples where scorn of death is the result of noble unselfishness: the famous Iberian *devotio*, namely the consecrated loyalty to a chief and the promise made to sacrifice one's life for him, or the case of the crucified Cantabrian prisoners who sang victory hymns on the cross. Trogus Pompeius notes as a special characteristic of the Spaniards that their minds are as well prepared for death as their bodies are for abstinence and toil (*corpora ad inediam laboremque, animi ad mortem parati*). Frequently indeed they have been known to die under torture rather than reveal a secret, preferring to keep silence than to save their life. Tacitus, a century later than Trogus, gives a particular instance; namely that of the rural Arevacan[2] from Tiermes who died under torture, shouting his refusal to reveal the names of certain conspirators. Life is not the

---

[1] A Greek geographer who lived at the end of the first century B.C.
[2] *Arévacos*, a Celtiberian tribe living in the actual province of Soria. Its capital was Numantia.

supreme boon. The ancient Spaniard sacrificed his life with patriotic enthusiasm, as in the case of the Cantabrians on the cross and the Numantians in their collective suicide. They sacrificed their life in order to accomplish the high duties of loyalty, not only individual but also national and international, as in the case of the sacrifice by the Saguntines. In these and other cases we do not know definitely what religious, political or social principles were responsible for this attitude of preferring death to other penalties, especially to the loss of liberty. But in all these instances we see traces of something akin to stoical doctrine. Seneca exhorts men to suicide as a liberation. Death is not to be feared; it is the end of all evils and the beginning of true freedom in eternity.

FAME

Both in the dimness of primitive times and in the clear light of modern days we find the truth of the saying of Trogus: *animi ad mortem parati*. Death is accepted as the beginning of survival in another higher life.

On the threshold of the great Spanish historic age Jorge Manrique[1] reveals calmly and serenely an attitude to death which draws distinctions between three lives; first of all temporal life which perishes; then the life of fame which is more enduring and more glorious than the life of the body; lastly eternal life, which is the crowning of the other two. Now these two lives after death are as consciously felt by every Spaniard to-day as in the past, and so intense is his awareness that it contrasts with the attitude of neighbouring races. With regard to the second life, that of fame, it is significant how the ideology of the Spanish soldier differed from that of the Italian in the early quarrels that took place between the leaders of both peoples, who served under Alfonso V of Aragon. We have accounts of one of these arguments which took place before the Magnanimous King in 1420. The Spaniards reproached the Italians for their slackness in fighting, and for the fact that so few died in their battles; whereat the great

---

[1] Jorge Manrique (1440–1478), knight of the Order of Santiago, engaged in the political struggles at the beginning of the reign of the Catholic Monarchs. His greatest poetical work is the elegy, *Coplas por la muerte de su padre*, 1467, very famous even to-day in Spain.

condottiere Braccio da Montone[1] replied, rebuking the Spaniards for their loutish fierceness: 'You think it more honourable to allow yourselves to be cut to pieces by the enemy than to escape with your lives and reserve yourselves for the day of revenge.'

Let us not consider those words as those of a typical condottiere devoid of warlike and patriotic spirit. The French, who abounded in both, yet noted the same tendency when they refused to fight the troops of the Great Captain, saying: 'Those mad Spaniards value a little honour more than a thousand lives and are incapable of enjoying this life.' This judgement shows how closely related Spanish idealism is to the sober austerity which we considered as the basis of the Spanish character. The tendency to set little value upon the pleasures of life, whether accompanied or not by noble aspirations, persists as a fundamental trait, with the result that the second life praised by Jorge Manrique, that of fame and honour, is not in Spain reserved merely for the illustrious hero, but is the stimulus for all men. Every knight aspires as Don Juan Manuel[2] did to win the guerdon of fame, for then mankind will say of him: 'The man died, but not his name' (*murió el hombre, mas no su nombre*); a motto which later became the heraldic device, *Muera el hombre y viva el nombre* (let the man die, but the name survive). This happened not only in those centuries when great national enterprises gave a high, coherent purpose to the wills of all. Quevedo in his Epistle to the Count-Duke Olivares[3] lamented the disappearance of the ancient valour:

> The luminous freedom of the spirit that refused to prolong life a day
> Once Death with honour showed the way.

But valour had not entirely perished. Even in periods of decline there are many unknown heroes who will face with unbowed heads death with honour on the altar of their ideals, and, as

---

[1] Braccio da Montone (1368–1424), lord of Perugia and a great part of Umbria. Ruled Rome for seventy days in 1417; in 1420 commanded the militia of Queen Joan of Naples (1414–1435) who adopted as successor Alfonso V the Magnanimous, King of Aragon.

[2] Grandson of King Ferdinand III, the most powerful noble in Castile, author of the book of exemplary tales, *El Conde Lucanor*, written about 1330.

[3] Conde Duque de Olivares, famous minister of Philip IV from 1621 to 1643, was pictured several times by Velázquez. The epistle of Quevedo was written in 1624.

Trogus said, men ready for death may be found even when they have lost all hope in the result of their self-sacrifice, as for instance in cases where war is waged against hopeless odds to the death of the last man.

This persistent longing for a second life and survival through honourable fame which absorbs the Spaniard reaches its purest and most complete fulfilment in religion.

RELIGION

A motto frequently used by the soldiers of the Counter-Reformation was: 'Give your life for honour, and give both, honour and life, for God.' By these words we see how the three lives which had been relatively appraised by Jorge Manrique were at that time present in the mind of every Spaniard and similarly appraised. All knew that in the end it was for God that the soldier sacrificed his life. Tansillo[1] in the three sonnets he wrote in memory of the huge heap of unburied bones lying on the Dalmatian shore—the bones of the ·3,000 defenders of Castel-novo[2] in 1539—celebrates the glory won on earth by those heroes of Iberia, but he adds that they won the supreme crown because they had sold dearly their perishable lives in order to buy eternal life. This third life to which religion guides mankind surpasses all the joys of earthly life, and it not infrequently happens that in the midst of this life's troubles the longing for death grows to a high pitch of exaltation, for to die will be to cross the threshold to a higher existence. This was how it appeared to Doctor Villalobos[3] when he wrote: 'Come now, gentle death, and give me freedom.' This thought of death, which is thirst for immortality, is the profound concern of the Spanish people and has been noted in its various aspects by our writers, but here it concerns us only as the ultimate basis of religion and in so far as the latter influences civil life.

[1] Luigi Tansillo (1510–1568), poet who served under the Viceroy of Naples, Don Pedro de Toledo, and fought against the Turks. Author of a famous poem, *Le lagrime di S. Pietro*, 1539.

[2] Castelnovo in the Bocche di Cattaro in Yugoslavia was a Turkish military base. Captured by the Venetians and the Spaniards in 1538, it was defended by the Spaniards and recaptured by Barbarossa, 10 August, 1539.

[3] Francisco de Villalobos, 1473–1549, doctor at the court of Charles V. The poem quoted was written by him on the occasion of the death of the Empress Isabel in Toledo, 1539.

When considering the general effects produced by deeply-rooted religious feeling we must note that it is the most powerful force for correcting the Spanish individual's disinclination to make concessions to the common welfare. A Spaniard usually does not trouble himself with duties or generosities of a social character beyond those inspired by charity towards his neighbour, and these he generally performs, not owing to his direct love for God and his neighbour, but rather owing to his desire to reap his merited reward in the life to come. As a result, therefore, the only people charged with giving effect to the charitable impulses of the individual in the direction of social welfare were the religious institutions. They, as was natural, interested themselves above all in the charitable aspect of their mission, but neglected other more worldly aspects, as has frequently been noted in the sphere of education. Owing to the policy of granting this exclusive credit to the religious institutions their number multiplied out of all proportion, and so likewise did the numbers of clerics and friars, a fact which was deplored by the political pamphleteers of the seventeenth century. Canon Fernández Navarrete devoted six Discourses to the evils caused to the monarchy by the excessive number of religious foundations and the multitude of secular priests. Saavedra Fajardo also referred to 'the devout prodigality' which impoverishes the people and its ruler owing to the excessive number of pious legacies. This excess continued in the following centuries; Jovellanos, for instance, points out as a grave economic evil the mortmain due to the 'countless foundations of convents, colleges, brotherhoods, guardianships, chaplaincies, anniversaries which sprang from the generosity of wealthy souls at their hour of agony'. It is clear that this excess could not be easily remedied, for this deep-rooted habit of devoting private charity to religious objects is also due to the definite distrust which every benefactor feels towards charitable organizations run by laymen, for they are sure to be as inefficient in social questions as he is himself, and thus he has no alternative but to place all his confidence in religious bodies.

This beneficial action exercised by Spanish religious sentiment in overcoming the lack of a collective spirit extended its influence also by giving a moral tone to civic behaviour. But here, too, we must note certain deficiencies. The Spaniard, owing to his customary disregard for ultimate perfection, is inclined to pay scant heed to strictly ethical standards. Content with natural moderation and simplicity of behaviour, he has no scruples about breaking the moral law more or less. When the decline was beginning in the golden centuries we find Simon Contarini, the Venetian ambassador at the court of the very pious monarch Philip III, noting one blatant contradiction in the Spaniards: 'They are,' he says, 'essentially Catholic in religion but by no means moral in their conduct.' Even if we discount this dogmatic assertion, it is quite true that we do at certain moments of political life meet this contradiction. It is disquieting that at times of great religious fervour, as, for instance, in the reactionary movements of Ferdinand VII in 1814 and 1823, the Spanish people, while experiencing a revival of patriotism through religion, did not follow its dictates of mercy and cease ruthlessly suppressing their political opponents, nor did they learn from it the principles of integrity which would guide them in administering the State.

Leaving aside the power religion has over the individual, its influence in public life appears as paramount on many vital occasions in Spanish history. At the beginning, the Councils of Toledo intervened under the Visigothic monarchy, guiding and moderating wisely the actions of the State, elaborating an admirable system of laws, and inspiring the government with noble politico-juridical principles, which are in contrast to the crude barbarity of the other Germanic kingdoms. But at the end of this period when there was a decline, the ecclesiastical element found itself so directly entangled in party struggles that when the catastrophe came both State and Church fell victims, one disappearing altogether and the other submitting to the Mozarabic domination.

The pure unfettered religious spirit which had been preserved in the north gave impetus and national aims to the Reconquest. Without its strength of purpose Spain would have given up in despair all resistance and would have become denationalized. In the end it would have become Islamized as did all the other provinces of the Roman Empire in the east and south of the Mediterranean. In the period from the eighth to the tenth centuries Islam appeared so immensely superior in power and culture to the West that it was amazing that Spain did not succumb as did

Syria and Egypt when they were Arabized, in spite of their more advanced Hellenistic culture; and as did Libya, Africa and Mauritania, likewise Arabized. What gave Spain her exceptional strength of collective resistance and enabled her to last through three long centuries of great peril was her policy of fusing into one single ideal the recovery of the Gothic states for the fatherland and the redemption of the enslaved churches for the glory of Christianity. This fusion of ideals was solemnly declared as a national aim in the *Epítome Ovetense* of the ninth century.

The Spanish religious spirit reached its zenith in the sixteenth and seventeenth centuries. Then it could count on a ruling minority which included men of highest worth in the nation, theologians who were able to intervene decisively in the Council of Trent and serve as leaders of learning in the European universities; mystical writers, ascetics and scripturists who were of the greatest produced by any country; poets who succeeded in interesting the whole people in the deepest problems of grace and free-will, in the most recondite questions of scholasticism as well as in the most subtle allegories of religious history. This great growth of religion had a political aspect that was of cardinal importance, namely, that it arose in a moment of national adversity. The Renaissance strengthened the spirit of nationality in the modern states and caused each of them to look exclusively to their own interests without any consideration for the spirit of Catholic unity upheld by the Middle Ages but now cracking and splitting asunder. Spain was the only country that carried on its inveterate mediaeval purpose and identified its own national aims with the universal aims of Christianity, taking them as her own from the reign of Ferdinand the Catholic, who, as Gracián said, 'knew how to join earth to heaven'. What Ferdinand began was afterwards developed by Spain in the magnificent outburst of enthusiasm of the Counter-Reformation when she devoted her entire life and energies to urging on in Europe the Catholic movement of reconstruction.

Once the bond of unity was broken there entered the new Renaissance doctrine of Reason of State. Every prince who was a reader of Tacitus and Machiavelli believed the interests of his State to be superior to all moral reasons, but Spain did not believe that there was any contradiction between her interests and religious precepts. The Christianization of the Reason of State which had been theoretically initiated in Italy by Botero[1] as a work of the Counter-Reformation, was afterwards a subject of general interest in Spain in the works of López Bravo, Saavedra Fajardo, Blázquez Mayoralgo and Gracián. All contradict Machiavelli yet all select one of the heroes of the Florentine secretary, namely Ferdinand the Catholic, as the 'great oracle of the Reason of State'. Thus, although in these treatises (as in Botero) we find various quasi-Machiavellian maxims peering out here and there from the purest doctrine of Christian and pagan authors, yet the evangelical law is essentially maintained. All those treatises were written when Philip IV was called 'the Great', in order to hide the beginning of decline which was already making itself felt. The fact is that even beneath the indolent Catholicism of 'the Great', Spain continued firm in her determination to join earth and heaven and clung desperately to the religious ideal she had created.

Although not on the same great scale, the superimposition of the religious ideal on political life could still be observed at a later date in many cases, and when we come to the War of Independence this superimposition becomes of the highest significance, for it contributed effectively to the strength and unity of the country. Afterwards, when in Spain national unity ceased to be identified with Catholic unity, this identification still remained as the essential aim of a great section of the Spanish people.

---

[1] Giovanni Botero (1533–1617), secretary to Cardinal St Charles Borromeo in Milan. His chief work, *Della Ragion di Stato*, was published in Venice 1589.

Chapter III

Individualism

THE INDIVIDUAL AND THE COMMUNITY

The Spaniard is inclined not to feel a sense of solidarity with the community except in so far as it will bring him immediate advantages, for he will always neglect indirect or future benefits. Hence he is rather indifferent to the welfare of the community or its problems, but in compensation he possesses a lively perception of his own individual case as well as that of his neighbour. This over-valuation of the individual has direct bearing upon the two cardinal principles of communal life: justice which regulates it and selection which divides it into hierarchies.

JUSTICE

Spanish literature in its most popular and most representative types has always betrayed an interest in juridical questions. The national drama continually brings the idea of justice to bear upon the most powerful dramatic situations, especially when justice is carried out, not according to the letter of the law, but for the benefit of individual cases; we come across terrible sentences in consequence of monstrous outrages; judgements like that of Solomon in which free will, outside all written law, enables the equitable decision to emerge triumphant from the difficulties that beset it; or again we find the solemn justification of rebellion against a tyrant, or of the formal illegality of a just sentence (*El Mejor Alcalde, el Rey*[1]; *Audiencias del Rey Pedro*; *Fuenteovejuna*; *Peribáñez, El Alcalde de Zalamea*).

Mediaeval epic poetry had created various scenes dealing with questions of law and justice which became famous and were used repeatedly up to modern times, as for instance, the challenge

[1] *El Mejor Alcalde, el Rey*, etc., plays by Lope de Vega and Calderón.

of Zamora,[1] the Oath at Santa Gadea,[2] the Cortes of Toledo.[3] These scenes were genuinely Spanish, for they did not adapt themselves in any way to the literary pattern brought into fashion by the celebrated and masterly French Epic. In fact, they broke this model and dramatized poetically conflicts of public and private law in which respect for justice prevails over military force or over the passion of vengeance which was then so strong. The *Romancero*, too, is so packed with legal saws and instances that Joaquín Costa[4] gathered them together and produced therefrom a complete corpus of legal usage. Some of those literary themes certainly sprang from historical fact; as, for instance, the oath at Santa Gadea which resembles another significant one in the history of the Kingdom of Aragon, namely, the Compromise of Caspe[5]—an arbitral decision which prevented a war of dynastic succession.

In history every period of prosperity is marked by a strengthening of justice and the opposite is the case in periods of decline. This contrast is abundantly clear in the most radical of the changes that have been registered in Spanish history. A transformation such as that which took place in the entire national life when, after the disastrous period of Henry IV, the Catholic Monarchs came to the throne, can only be explained by regarding it as a reinstauration of justice. In those days it was a long and wearisome task to secure the proper functioning of justice, and almost all the first seven years of the new reign were devoted to it. Most of the time was spent in curbing the knights who had be-

---

[1] *El Reto de Zamora* (The Challenge of Zamora), an epic story dealing with the treacherous murder of King Sancho II in 1072, and the duel or judicial challenge which ensued in order to prove whether the Council of Zamora was innocent or culpable of the murder of the king.

[2] The oath at S. Gadea, a famous scene in the epic poem when Alfonso VI swears that he was not guilty of the murder of his brother Sancho II.

[3] The Cortes of Toledo, principal scene in the *Poema del Cid* where the Infantes of Carrión are tried for having abandoned shamefully their wives, the daughters of the Cid.

[4] Joaquín Costa (1846–1911), Aragonese jurist, sociologist and politician. The works quoted here are: *Concepto del derecho en la poesía popular española; Oligarquía y caciquismo*, 1901; *Reconstitución y europeización de España*.

[5] When the King of Aragon, Martin I, died in 1410 there were six claimants to the throne; in order to prevent strife between the partisans of the three parliaments of Aragon, Catalonia and Valencia, each parliament named three delegates or *compromisarios* (one of them was S. Vincent Ferrer from Valencia) who met at Caspe (March–June 1412). Ferdinand, the Infante of Castile, was elected and crowned at Saragossa two months later.

come highway robbers, and other petty tyrants whose hands were against all men. After those seven years came a long period when there were less disturbances, but there still existed the need for strict control in order to preserve law and order. The transformation which had taken place was clearly visible in all public administration and the chroniclers note it. Before this period not only civil but even criminal justice was for sale. Every judge would repeat one of the favourite aphorisms of Henry IV, namely that the corpse of an executed criminal is worth nothing, and so it is preferable to free criminals from the gallows for money. Afterwards as a contrast to the corrupt maxim of Henry IV we have the case of the noble-born highwayman from Medina, who, to save his life, undertook to pay over forthwith 40,000 doubloons for the war against the Moors. The Catholic Queen, however, rejected the offer and had him executed, but refused to confiscate his goods according to the criminal code of the day, 'that people might not think that she had ordered justice to be done because she coveted his possessions'.

Thus the Crown, even though it was already firmly implanted in the minds of the people, yet wished more and more to rely upon public opinion and promote a spirit of confidence and optimism. This the Catholic Monarchs did achieve decisively, and every one praised what Vespasiano da Bistici[1] calls the *inviolabile giustizia* of Ferdinand whereby he satisfied both rich and poor, and the severe and inflexible sense of duty of Isabel when she expressed pleasure at seeing every one in his right place: 'men-at-arms in the field, bishops in their pontificals, robbers on the gallows'. This inexorable and incorruptible justice brought about a golden age which was perpetually remembered in successive centuries as the most prosperous era of the nation.

This devotion to just government, once it was established and practised with truly religious zeal, continued under the great succeeding monarchs throughout the whole sixteenth century, its special note being its refusal to give heed to personal considerations. It was not only in the autos-da-fé where, in the sacred interests of religion, a Marquis de Poza was degraded, or where Doña Ana Enríquez, the daughter of the Marquis de Alcañices

[1] Vespasiano da Bistici (1421–1498), famous Florentine bookseller who was associated with all the men of letters of his day, among them Spaniards. His principal work is *Vite di uomini illustri*.

appeared in the *sambenito* (penitential gown) and was condemned to prison amidst general commiseration, for all were moved by her great beauty and noble bearing. Many scions of the noblest houses suffered exile or prison for common offences, even when the accused was the Duke of Alba, the Count of Tendilla, the Duke of Osuna or the Count of Paredes.

This stern integrity prevailed in the early years of the seventeenth century and in Philip III's reign a counsellor and almoner of the King of France observed in his travels through Spain that the laws were, without distinction of classes, better observed there than in France, where all was permitted to the nobles, even crime, whereas in Spain a duke's son suffered the full rigour of the law, and in the case of gentlemen who fought a duel, the penalty was to have a hand nailed to a pillory in the plaza, no matter how richly dressed they were. In the same period Pinheiro da Veiga[1] at the Court of Valladolid observed that it was the memory of Philip II, a true priest of justice, that caused justice and its ministers to be not only feared and respected, but even adored in Castile.

This deep concern with legality affected the very foundations of the State which had expanded owing to the recent advances in geographical discovery. In the reign of Charles V lawyers debated for years the legal problem of how to incorporate into western civilization a vast number of peoples who were living in a state of nature. At the very moment when the ancient notion of European history-laden Empire was dying out, there arose the Spanish empire, without history, the first one of modern times not anchored to Roman and mediaeval law, but eager to discover new standards of natural and international law. Hence the opposition which existed between the humanitarian cleric Las Casas and the humanist scholar Ginés de Sepúlveda,[2] both of them inhuman, for the former made all colonization impossible, and the latter permitted it to flourish under tyranny. This chaotic and

[1] Tomé Pinheiro da Veiga (1571–1656), native of Coimbra, resided in Valladolid when Philip III had his court there and wrote a diary of his stay (April–June 1605) under the title *Fastiginia o fastos geniaes*.

[2] Juan Ginés de Sepúlveda (1490–1574), humanist, chronicler of Charles V. His work, *Democrates sive de justis belli causis apud indos*, upholding the right in law of the Spaniards to make war on the Indians and subjugate them, attacks Las Casas who held that it was lawful only to negotiate peacefully and from equal to equal with the chiefs of the Indians. The polemics on the right of domination over the Indians took place chiefly between the years 1542–1551.

misleading position was remedied by the great theologians and jurists such as Francisco de Vitoria, Diego Covarrubias and Domingo de Soto, who raised the whole controversy to a higher and more serene level of doctrine, this enabling the necessary guardianship to be applied to primitive peoples. At the same time, with a spirit of impartiality, they dispelled the two ideas which had been the mainstay of the mediaeval empire, by denying that ascendancy over the whole world was possessed either by the Pope, who had made the celebrated Donation, or by the Emperor, who at the moment reigned in Spain. Here we had the unusual occurrence of a State undertaking to discuss with itself the legality of its own dominion. From this lofty spirit of justice sprang the exemplary Laws of the Indies, which are a model of modern methods of colonization never surpassed; their noble spirit may be summed up in the ordinance of Philip II which directed that any injuries and ill treatment inflicted by Spaniards on the Indians should be more heavily punished than if those crimes had been committed against Spaniards, and he declared that they were to be considered crimes against the State.

EQUITY AND ARBITRARINESS

This radiant sense of justice which is reflected in the above examples is united to feelings of moderation inspired by the anxiety to temper the rigidity of the abstract law to the individual case.

It is worthy of note in the works of Saint Isidore, the Conciliary Canons and the *Fuero Juzgo*, how much the principle of *aequitas* and *pietas* prevails as a means of reducing the severity of punishments. And by extending the notion that the general written law is unjust in many concrete cases, primitive Castile revolted even against the *Fuero Juzgo* when considered as an inviolable law, and decided to submit to judges who would judge according to their own idea of the equitable principles required by each individual case. It is in this way that Castile comes into being in an impulse of individualism over against the Kingdom of León. It is due to freedom of will, equity and compassion that the idea of pardon is given such a prominent place in our Spanish penal code. A French writer, Monsieur Legendre, although a fervent Catholic, considers that the traditional collective pardon given on Good Friday is contrary to the duty which society has of punishing the guilty. From early days it has been observed how easily the Spaniard is moved to pity and sympathy for the man who pays the penalty: he may even take the side of the criminal and help him to escape, as Don Quixote did with the galley slaves. In fact all look upon one who has come within the range of the law more as a victim of misfortune than as a dangerous criminal. This is another instance of how the interests of the individual are set before those of the community.

This tendency may, sometimes, lead to dangerous extremes. The unvarying justice of the great periods, which was considered superior to that prevailing in other countries, disappears in periods of decline and gives way to an inferior state of affairs, likewise noted in comparison with foreign countries. At such a time the Spaniard does not recognize the common good of society except in very special circumstances. He refuses to bear in mind that the individual cannot avoid the repercussions caused by the vicissitudes of the community. This individualism then is far removed from that of the Anglo-Saxon, who for ever looks to social justice as the necessary support for the interests of each individual. And since a society which has degenerated in such a way is nothing but the sum total of individuals, the laws governing that society will also disintegrate into a series of individual cases, and the peculiar circumstances of each case will be considered exceptions to the general rule. The result will be a general lack of respect for the law, whether because it is considered inequitable as regards the case in point, or because of the unconscious contempt for the public good felt by the individual. 'Laws', it is said, 'are only made for the pleasure of breaking them'; a degrading pleasure indeed and one which is principally enjoyed by rulers themselves in a degenerate age, when any authority, be he high or low, thinks that his dignity suffers if he submits to the rules followed by the common citizens, and starting from this maxim believes that he will lose his main chance if he does not exercise the abusive prerogatives to which his public office lends itself. Caciquism[1] or the petty-boss system organized

---

[1] *Cacique*, a word derived from the Indians of Cuba and very frequently used in the fifteenth century to describe a person who uses undue political influence in a locality or region; *caciquismo*, a word admitted into the Spanish Academy Dictionary in 1884, signifies the grave defects of the parliamentary system in Spain. The

the most shameless illegality under the motto: 'Go as far as injustice for your friend and refuse justice to your enemy' (*Al amigo hasta lo injusto, y al enemigo ni lo justo*). Similar arbitrary methods, though on a less systematic scale, have been frequently noted throughout Spanish history, as the Duke of Maura has shown conclusively.

The total lack of civic spirit in the depressed periods of history is shown clearly by the falsification of votes and the jerrymandering of elections. This evil does not date from the period of caciquism, when such arbitrary practices aroused great anxiety among the foremost thinkers and politicians, but from the Middle Ages when the kings and grandees brought pressure to bear upon the cities in the matter of the appointment of Procurators to the Cortes. In those days and as late as the seventeenth century they made a practice of bribing these Procurators, inducing them to be generous at public expense and to impose burdens upon the people. In the constitutional period, however, it is clear that the Spanish people never succeeded in making its will felt through universal suffrage and had no belief in it.

Amongst the other means of expression it preferred the *Pronunciamiento* as a regular institution. In the first third of the nineteenth century *Pronunciamientos* begin to be the order of the day and the necessary instrument for the constitutionalists who had no legal means of defending the introduction of suffrage. When later there were both Constitution and suffrage, Progressives and Moderates alike launched their *Pronunciamientos*, from Espartero and Narváez[1] to Prim. Generals, who, in addition, were deputies to the Cortes, wished to express the opinion of their own party, not in the Cortes or in elections, but by force of arms. On the other hand when the politicians of the Restoration came into power, they showed no greater belief in suffrage, but adapted it to their own convenience and corrupted it by means of caciquism. And the Spanish people remained indifferent in face of this falsification of their vote, not only because they lacked civic

---

arbitrary behaviour of the caciques perverts the elections and the application of the law. This national problem culminated in the publication of Costa's book '*Oligarquía y caciquismo*', 1901, and when Maura, who was Minister of the Interior in 1902, published what he called *Descuaje de* (or Disintegration of) *caciquismo*.

[1] General Baldomero Espartero, victor in the first Carlist war 1839, and later his opponent General Ramón María Narváez were alternately the masters of Spanish politics between 1837 and 1868.

sense, but also because they were given a kind of universal franchise which did not arouse their interest. It is strange that nobody suggested as a remedy for this state of affairs the possibility of adapting to Spanish needs foreign methods of franchise, in a way which would suit the extremely individualistic nature of the Spaniard, always inclined to disregard collective interests unless they are concerned with immediate objectives of daily life.

GOODWILL AND ENVIOUSNESS

One special characteristic of the opposition between justice and arbitrariness is that existing between selective appreciation and envy. Generous esteem of others might be personified in Cervantes, in whose mind all the reverses of life, all the unjust buffetings of chance arouse no resentful or rancorous thought but rather inexhaustible optimism and benevolent irony, the unfailing abnegation of Don Quixote, the kindly roguishness of Sancho, who is prepared to find good people even in hell.

This benevolent appreciation of the world has as its opposite the attitude of envious disparagement, which is lack of clear vision, an intellectual blindness rendering a man incapable of seeing merits in any one but himself. In most cases it degenerates into envy which is aversion to the excellent qualities of others and a reaction excited by the painful realization of one's own inferiority.

It is due to an excess of individualism and a deficiency in social values that envy is so widespread in Spain. Gracián calls it *malignidad hispana* (Spanish maliciousness) and he indicates the master qualities (*primores*) which will enable the Great Man to attenuate the attacks of this malevolent spirit. To the passion of envy Count Gondomar, an acute observer, attributed in 1606 strong literary repercussions, for he believed that the reason why no historical reports were being written was due to 'the envy and rivalry existing between Spaniards who believed that each one deprived himself of whatever praise or merit he allowed to his neighbour'. An infinite number of discourses and discussions on this passion by Spanish and Ibero-american authors could be collected. Foreign authors, too, have continually noted its prevalence and have pointed out the truth of the famous caricature of the three greased poles in the fair, each with its prize at the top.

The first is a French pole, and the competitor who climbs up does so amid the encouraging applause of the audience: the second is an English one, and the public watches the climber in silent rapt attention: the last is Spanish, but here the spectators yell at the man who tries to climb up and one even pulls him by the legs to prevent him from reaching the top.

The life story of every celebrated Spaniard has to note these envious obstructions, and the first separate biography in Spanish literature, that of the Cid, gives repeatedly details of this perpetual struggle between generosity and malevolence. The Cid is an object of envy to the grandees at court, to his own relations, to the King himself. But although driven into exile on several occasions he steadfastly refuses to harbour thoughts of resentment or revenge, and behaves with great magnanimity. He never weakens in his resolve not to use the right granted to him by the *fuero de los hijosdalgo* (privilege of nobility), whereby it was lawful for him to make war on the king who had exiled him, but uses his arms in the national war and offers his conquests to the ungrateful king. This generous behaviour is confirmed by history and idealized by poets as a characteristic Spanish trait, and it contrasts with the usual behaviour attributed by the ancient epic poetry of all peoples to the exiled vassal who is for ever at war with his king.

The reverse of the generosity of the Cid, namely the envy of the king which was denounced by the ancient biographer, is of great significance. Although Alfonso VI was a king of eminent qualities and in the first period of his reign won brilliant successes, nevertheless he exemplifies the essentially Spanish saying of Calderón:

No man so hapless lives but has one to envy him;
No man so full of honours but has one he envies more.

Alfonso the fortunate envies the Cid but will not make use of his services, and this rebuff it was which decided the fate of the monarch, for in the second part of his life he lingered for twenty-three consecutive years in misfortune, meeting with defeat after defeat at the hands of the Almorávides,[1] while the Cid whom he

[1] Almorávides, a name taken by a nomadic Berber tribe of the Sahara which built up an eastern African empire (1042–1147). In 1086 they invaded Moslem Spain, routing Alfonso VI in the battles of Zalaca or Sagrajas, 1086, Jaén, 1092,

had exiled went from triumph to triumph against those same invaders from Africa. Alfonso VI had the advantage of having inherited a kingdom which was on the ascendant grade as a result of the exploits of his predecessors to the throne, but nevertheless his fortunes declined when, prompted by envy, he gave way to his impulse and exiled the hero. The opposite course was followed by the Catholic Monarchs. They came to the throne after several decadent reigns, especially the last one, but far from rebuffing the famous hero, they endeavoured constantly to discover unknown heroes, and, as a result of their efforts, Spain's fortunes, which had been at their nadir, soared to their zenith; a country which had been reduced to a heap of ruins became the most powerful state in Europe.

FROM HENRY IV TO THE CATHOLIC MONARCHS

Alonso de Palencia, the first to stress the change which occurred at the death of Henry IV and the succession of Ferdinand and Isabel, compares the transformation to the sun suddenly piercing the clouds after a long storm. According to Modesto Lafuente[1] the social anarchy of the previous period disappeared 'as though by enchantment', and the corpse-like nation became a robust healthy body. But this transformation did not occur with such suddenness; there was no such magic resurrection when the Catholic sovereigns mounted the throne. What happened was that a period of patient reconstruction ensued in which the most important part was, as we said before, the restoration of justice.

Justice, however, by itself would explain public well-being, but not great prosperity. We must specify another decisive peculiarity in the methods of governing adopted by those sovereigns, one which among all the qualities attributed to them was the principal cause of their extraordinary success, namely the spirit of selection, which after all is another form of justice.

We have denied that the transformation which took place at the coming of Ferdinand and Isabel was sudden, but neither was it very slow. It took place among those very generations which

---

Consuegra, 1097, and Ucles 1108. The Cid drove back in confusion a great army of Almorávides at the gates of Valencia and destroyed another big army at the battle of Cuarte, 1094.

[1] Author of a *Historia general de España* in thirty volumes, 1850–1859.

had lived amid the corruption of Henry IV's reign. This means that among those generations there existed certain healthy elements which afterwards co-operated towards the rise to prosperity. On the one hand there were the resolute people who grouped themselves together into 'brotherhoods' to chastise lawlessness, first in Castile, then in Biscay, Galicia and Aragon; on the other hand there were certain grandees who gathered together in plotting bands, insisting on reform both in the government and social habits. Nevertheless, all those valuable elements proved ineffective since they were passed over and could take no part in the direction of national life. Those worthy grandees who gathered in Burgos in 1464 put forward as the cause of misgovernment the fact that public charges were 'sold to the highest bidder', and that they were always held by 'inefficient persons of little learning'. Many other witnesses of those days refer to this faulty method of selection: Gómez Manrique[1] says that it was the order of the day in a kingdom which was in decline and handed over to covetous self-seekers, where the fool is appointed mayor and the best candidates are passed over:

> The best are of less worth,
> Mark what a government:
> That the good should be governed
> By those who are not so!
> The wise should flee away
> When madmen rule the day,
> For when the blind are leaders
> Woe to those who follow after!

From this country where fools, madmen and degenerates ruled, from among those nobles who served only to deceive the people with false promises, sprang those who shortly afterwards were to devote themselves to enterprises of high renown and lead the nation from its lowest depths to the highest peak of its historical destiny. The only explanation for this radical and relatively rapid change lies in the scrupulous system of selection mentioned above, which enabled the rulers to extract from a spoiled mixture the uncontaminated leaven. Had they not at the height of their power

---

[1] Gómez Manrique (1413–91), Castilian noble, uncle of Jorge Manrique. The poem referred to is entitled *Querella de la gobernación* and was written during the youth of the poet in the reign of Henry IV (1454–1474).

persevered in this method of careful selection, those in the country who wished for reform might have succeeded in grouping themselves effectively and managed to establish a government. But though it would have been an improvement on conditions under Henry IV, it would not have given rise to the astonishingly rapid prosperity which actually did take place.

FERDINAND AND ISABEL TOGETHER

It would be necessary to search contemporary documents for details concerning this selective work, for the historians have not investigated the question. Only one ancient chronicler, Galíndez de Carvajal,[1] drew attention to the great importance of the subject and gave general information on it. Galíndez attributes to both monarchs the rules which were adopted, but one suspects that this was due to the fact that Isabel had ordered her chroniclers not to speak of her alone but to employ always the double expression 'the King and Queen', and Hernando del Pulgar,[2] who was wearied by the usage of this rigid formula, made fun of it by entitling an imaginary chapter of his history as follows: 'On such and such a day the King and Queen gave birth to a daughter'. In one case, at least, as we shall see, certain procedure which Galíndez attributed to both monarchs is by another author (and an Aragonese to boot) attributed to Isabel only; and by the way, we should note that Castiglione[3] limits his encomiums to the Queen alone. Nevertheless, in support of Galíndez we should remember that Machiavelli praises Ferdinand for his subtle discernment of men, and it is well known that this great king distinguished himself by his power of selecting the assistants he needed for carrying out his own system of government. We may thus reach the conclusion that the skill in selection was more the quality of Isabel and was applied by her scrupulously and religiously to all questions in life. The necessity for selection was a rule of conduct for her both in trifling as well as in important matters. Ferdinand, whose distinctive quality was his amazing

[1] Lorenzo Galíndez de Carvajal (1472–1532), jurist and historian, author of *Anales del reinado de los Reyes Católicos*.
[2] See note 1, p. 131.
[3] Baldassare Castiglione wrote a famous book *Il Cortigiano* between the years 1507 and 1513. He was Nuncio of Pope Clement VII at the court of Charles V in 1524 and died in Toledo, 1529.

clearness of vision in political matters, a quality which made him the first king in Christendom, was without doubt selective in all that concerned his political tasks, but in other matters he did not pay much attention to the worth or worthlessness of people, as we shall see. He admitted his inferiority in this point, and even in his great international undertakings made use of Isabel's wisdom, and she would point out to him the right man for the task. Castiglione was correct in saying that the principal dowry that Ferdinand had received in his marriage was not the kingdom of Castile but the talent of the Queen.

By this we do not intend to bring up once again the puerile problem which obsessed so many in the past and still does to-day, namely, which of the two monarchs was the greater, for the distribution of personal characteristics in this exceptional married couple was very complex. From our point of view it is evident that Ferdinand took part in the work of selection, and even in cases where his actual share was negligible, there was positive value in the fact that he trusted in the Queen's opinion and accepted it.

CHARACTERISTICS OF ISABEL'S SELECTION

When we discover details left by contemporary witnesses of the selective care taken by the Catholic Monarchs in appointments we find one detail of general character which presents the Queen to us in a predominant rôle. Count Baldassare Castiglione in the third book of 'Il Cortigiano' tells us of 'the divine manner of governing' of the Catholic Queen, saying that her will alone was equivalent to an order preventing any one from doing anything which might offend her, for all knew that her sense of justice was as ready to chastise as her sense of generosity was to reward, and he adds that all this depended upon 'the marvellous talent she possessed for discovering and selecting the most suitable men for the tasks she imposed upon them'. This sharp judgement of men which she constantly practised was lasting in its effects, for when Castiglione wrote more than twelve years after the death of the Catholic Queen he adds: 'In our days, all the celebrated men in Spain, no matter for what reason they were famous, were creations of Queen Isabel.'

All the life of this Queen was a perpetual process of selection carried out meticulously and scrupulously from childhood, when she managed to procure for herself, against the will of Henry IV, detailed information about her English, French and Aragonese suitors, and decided by herself alone to marry Ferdinand. And in this first selection she discovered truly the one person with whom she was able to share both actions and thoughts. Passing on now to more precise details, in the first place Galíndez de Carvajal tells us that the Catholic Monarchs, in dealing with questions of government, 'were more inclined to appoint prudent people suitable for their service, even though they were of middle rank, rather than those of noble houses'; that is to say, they avoided ancient deep-seated privileges and broadened the possibilities of election, thus building up an aristocracy of talent against the aristocracy of birth. This note by Galíndez can be illustrated by many examples. We may recall the case of Cisneros. This stubborn, cross-grained friar was, against his will, appointed by Isabel Archbishop of Toledo, but his appointment was against the wishes of Ferdinand, who wished the mitre to be given to his natural son the Archbishop of Saragossa. In spite of this Isabel decided that the see of Toledo should cease to be the exclusive patrimony of the noble clerics as it had been in the past. Had this decision not been taken Cisneros would not have been more than a friar of no importance, hidden away in some convent, and the princely funds of the archdiocese of Toledo would not have been applied to the conquest of Oran, the first step made by Spain in Africa, nor to the University of Alcalá, to the Polyglot Bible, which was the first application of modern philology to the text of the Scriptures, and to many other enterprises. Another important example may be given to illustrate the point made by Galíndez, namely the fact that the monarchs appointed to the Royal Council, the Chancery of Valladolid and the various special governmental commissions learned jurists, 'people midway between the great and the small, whose profession was to study law', as Diego Hurtado de Mendoza said. In other countries there was a general tendency to admit the middle class to take regular part in the government, but nowhere was this tendency so decisively marked as under the Catholic Sovereigns.

The most subtle stroke in this matter of selection, one that makes it no less difficult than profitable, is that the election or rejection be independent of services or disservices rendered. Galíndez notes that when any one asked for a post in justice, government or war, and pointed out the services he had rendered, or as it was said, 'his adhesion to authority', he received the answer that services were rewarded in other ways, as indeed they were, but that in matters of government it was necessary to consider only the business in hand and see to it that posts were efficiently held. 'Hence many were called from their homes who had no notion that they would be appointed, and this was the reason why those monarchs were well served, and their vassals were inclined to virtue.' Here we may recall how Ferdinand, through the wise though risky advice of the Queen, appointed as leader of the Aragonese expedition in Naples Gonzalo de Córdoba, the future Great Captain, who was a younger son of an Andalusian house, and could not claim to have performed great services, in fact none at all for the Crown of Aragon. To this we should add that they did not by any means count only upon their supporters, but took special care to use the services of former adversaries, as in the case of the Marquis of Cadiz, Rodrigo Ponce de León, who, though a staunch partisan of La Beltraneja[1] and the King of Portugal, yet, through the instrumentality of the Queen, was attracted and received with marked favour by both sovereigns. It was they who made him give up the fierce war which he and the Duke of Medinasidonia had been waging fruitlessly to their own destruction, and succeeded in persuading both to co-operate in the conquest of Granada, vying with each other in great exploits. In short, owing to the influence of the sovereigns, a period of noble rivalry succeeded one of hatred and envy.

The same insistence in making use of former enemies was shown by Isabel in her treatment of Carrillo, the Archbishop of Toledo. Although she was very jealous of her own royal dignity, yet she endured the slights she received from him, and out of magnanimity tried her best to placate (in vain, it is true) the ire of that prelate, who though stubborn and valiant was of limited

[1] La Beltraneja, nick-name given to Juana, the daughter of Henry IV, born in 1462, on the suspicion that she was not the daughter of the king but of Don Beltran de la Cueva. Henry IV declared the illegitimacy of Juana and recognized Isabel the Catholic as heiress to the throne in 1468; but in 1470 he named Juana. The wars of succession caused by this proclamation ended with the Battle of Toro, 1476, in which the King of Portugal, who had married Juana and upheld her rights, was defeated.

intelligence. Even the most adverse circumstances never confused the subtle judgement of the Queen in searching out and
making use of profitable material. Columbus, who had failed in
his schemes with various sovereigns, and who could not convince
any one, owing to his deficient knowledge of cosmography, and
his exorbitant ambition, found in Isabel one who appreciated in
him the extraordinary man of action, who was able to endure the
untold risks of an unique adventure.

With the patient tenacity of genius ('she was very hardworking
herself and very firm in her purpose') she kept a sharp look-out on
all sides for people to fill both high as well as humble posts. Fray
Juan de Santa María relates that once a piece of paper fell from
the Queen's hands; on it she had written in her own handwriting
the following reminder: 'The office of common crier must be
given to so-and-so, for he has the bigger voice.' Doubtless she was
determined to prevent some piece of petty jobbery.

This constant attention which the monarchs gave to every
detail was aided by a regular information service which they set
up. According to Galíndez 'they had persons of their own close
confidence, who travelled through the country finding out how it
was governed and how justice was administered, and what was
said about the ministers. These confidential agents brought back
to the monarchs special reports on what they noticed, and reme-
dies were found as dictated by necessity.' This diligent watchful-
ness is another essential point. Thanks to their continued perseverance in the task of selecting the holders of office, the Catholic
sovereigns managed to change the downward course which the
workings of envy had given to the nation during the preceding
reigns. The problem was, in each struggle which arose between
the selfish thoughtless man and the man with genuine civic sense,
to help the victory of the latter. In the fratricidal scene of
Montiel,[1] Rocaberti, by merely helping to turn over the two
brothers in their mortal struggle, when they fell to the ground,
had done enough to set up a new dynasty. In the hubbub of the
days of Henry IV the best men in the realm fought under hopeless conditions and were only a helpless minority. By a change in
the relative positions, it was possible for them to become a vic-

---

[1] Montiel in the province of Ciudad Real, was the place where in 1369 King
Peter the Cruel was killed in a hand-to-hand struggle with his bastard brother,
Henry. The dynasty of Trastamara begins with the latter.

torious majority. There was no attempt to create new personnel, nor was there any waiting for a new generation educated on new principles. Cisneros, the Marquis of Cadiz, the Great Captain, all were men whose characters had been formed in the society of Henry IV. Thus, from the lowest pitch of decline to the highest peak of prosperity of a people there is only one step, but a step that is truly difficult to make, as difficult, in fact, as it is to pull out of the quagmire of selfish personal aggrandisement and tread the firm ground of honour and duty. It is difficult to continue day after day constantly and inflexibly overcoming covetousness and ambition, scrutinizing and testing the great or small capacities of each candidate to discover the best place in which to put him, so that he may develop those capacities; and once that is done to protect him against the attacks of the envious, as Isabel had to do with the utmost diligence when her protégés were the victims of malicious slander. She would as willingly defend the Great Captain when he was in difficulties after Barletta,[1] as she would the poor town-crier with the bigger voice when he was about to be passed over.

A period of prosperity is not the mysterious result of a series of fortuitous circumstances. The plethora of great men at certain periods and the scarcity at others has been explained by the saying that nature has her alternating periods of fertile harvesting and restful fallow (W. Pinder). But this metaphor does not explain matters, for in this case we are not dealing with mysterious natural forces, but with historical causes and circumstances which may favour or retard the blossoming forth of the very best human capacities which lie beneath the surface of everyday life. These causes and circumstances indeed may at one moment select and encourage the growth of those capacities, at another moment they may destroy them. In the case of the Catholic Monarchs, in addition to considering the fermentation produced by the ideas of the Renaissance, which were spreading through Spain during all the fifteenth century, we must consider as the decisive element Isabel's genius for selecting the right man for the right job.

[1] Barletta, an Italian city in the province of Bari on the Adriatic, where in the war between the French and the Spanish for the kingdom of Naples the Great Captain was besieged for nine months (July 1502–April 1503). Afterwards he won the great battles of Cerignola and Garigliano.

Castiglione has a phrase which is most revealing in this connection: '*A' nostri tempi tutti gli uomini grandi di Spagna e famosi in qualsivoglia cosa, sono creati dalla regina Isabella.*'

The prosperity of Spain was not a product of natural forces plentifully disseminated, but was the result of pure human will, which spread through an uninterrupted series of effects. Every man chosen became in his turn an agent of selection, and this spread like a drop of oil on paper. The very names we have quoted bring back the memory of the courage inspired by the Great Captain in his followers; his speeches to his troops with their admiring references to the heroes of antiquity made all long to emulate those glorious exploits. Cisneros, too, is a proof of how strong is the power of attraction or repulsion wielded by the 'select' individual over the man of positive or of negative sign, as in the case of Nebrija. Nebrija had quarrelled with him over a difference of opinion with regard to the Polyglot Bible. Nevertheless, Cisneros welcomed him generously to Alcalá when he heard that he had been deprived of his chair at Salamanca, and persecuted by the Inquisition. He assigned to him a professorship worth 60,000 *maravedís* with 100 *fanegas* of bread, telling him 'to lecture or teach whatever subject he wished, and if he did not wish to lecture not to do so, for he did not give him this appointment to make him work, but as a reward for all that Spain owed him'. The reverse side of the medal appears when we note the mutual antipathy between Cisneros and the Archbishop of Santiago, Alonso de Fonseca, the second of those of that name, a man self-willed in everything, who actually excommunicated Cisneros. When Fonseca in 1506 passed on the Archbishopric to his son Alonso de Fonseca, the third of the name, with the consent of Ferdinand the Catholic, Cisneros censured the king for violating in such an outrageous manner all selective principles, saying: 'Sir, it seems that Your Highness has made of the archbishopric of Santiago a family inheritance, and I would fain know whether women are excluded from it.' The complaint did not cancel the arbitrary act but at least it produced great remorse in the king's conscience, and this itself was a guarantee against further errors. In a word, in spite of such blemishes, the 'divine manner of ruling' attributed to Isabel by Castiglione, and the practice of incorruptible justice and vigorous selection, created an atmosphere of optimism among the people, for each individual felt that he was allowed to give the best of himself; there was a general *afición a la virtud* (love of virtue), as Galíndez said, and the continual insistence on incorruptible justice produced a society which was well ordered according to its human possibilities, and in which all the first values in the nation were enabled to flourish.

Furthermore, the selective system is held firm by a keystone. Isabel did not make her chief appointments in haphazard fashion when the necessity arose, but prepared them carefully beforehand. Antonio Agustín relates that 'Queen Isabel had a book locked in a casket of which she alone had the key, and in that book she kept a list of names of the people who deserved to be appointed to bishoprics, councils, judgeships, governorships and other posts, and she received previous information against the occurrence of a vacancy.' Galíndez, as usual, attributes this practice to both sovereigns, saying that 'in order to be prepared when the time came for making appointments they had a book containing lists of the ablest and most deserving candidates for vacant posts, and the same for bishoprics and ecclesiastical dignities.' Every distrustful and envious governor, too, has his book but he imagines that, as there is always a surplus of office-seekers, he will have no difficulty in selecting, and so he notes down in the book only the people who are disloyal or to be avoided, so that he may reject them if they do apply for posts.

DECLINE OF ISABEL'S SELECTIVE SYSTEM

This Book of Capabilities must have seemed to the people to be an effective system, for the Cortes of Valladolid of 1537 begged Charles V to follow the example of his grandparents and gather together secret information concerning the qualities and merits of candidates for office, and they added: 'Such a book is all the more necessary as Your Majesty has more kingdoms and dominions.' Charles granted the petition and Juan Ginés de Sepúlveda relates how conscientiously the Emperor considered the matter of his appointments, what aversion he felt to men whose reputation was unfounded, and how he would prefer to appoint unknown persons about whom he had received good reports. By thus continuing the selective system Charles has been praised by historians as a ruler who knew how to find his collaborators and make the best use of their talents.

Philip II continued to use the Book with its list of eligible candidates for office, but nevertheless this great king, owing to his enormous power of work and his distrustful character, kept all to himself and gave scant trust to those he had appointed, so that on occasions he would favour men of mediocre talent or none at all. The reports by ambassadors or historians show us that Philip, though he made up for it by his good qualities and his lofty ideals, yet had in his nature a touch of the envy to which we referred before. According to these reports, Philip at times appointed president of some Council or mission an insignificant or foolish individual, and placed under him others of genuine merit, who would prevent any grave blunders being made. Thus, as the president was of no account whatever, the king's supreme directing hand could be all the more apparent to all and would meet with no obstacle. But this unfortunate system was applied even in the case of the Great Armada. The incapable Duke of Medinasidonia, although he insisted that he was utterly inexperienced in nautical matters, had to accept command over the greatest naval force that was ever mustered, at the supremely decisive moment for the Spanish empire and the Catholic Counter-Reformation. Under the useless Captain General were appointed expert commanders and admirals, whose advice, it was believed, would be followed by the prudent, docile Medinasidonia, but naturally such advisers were powerless to prevent the continuous vacillations and the countless obvious mistakes which led to the great disaster. Thus all the abnegation and sacrifice shown by the nation in this vital enterprise was frustrated more than by any other cause by a wrong appointment made by the king under the stress of envy.

The nomination of that grandee as commander of the 'Invincible Armada' is a proof that times had changed from the days when it was possible to appoint an unassuming younger son to the Naples enterprise or a humble friar to the archbishopric of Toledo. Among the experienced commanders who had been chosen to assist the incompetent chief, Philip did not try to select one who might become a future hero. He preferred that the God of armies should grant the triumph of his cause to a well-known incompetent, for there was no danger that glory would turn his head: this, doubtless, was what Philip felt in his mind, according to the interpretation of a sharp-witted Italian, who added that the king suffered from *la infirmità della sospetta* (suspicion sickness) for he showed himself in all things *assai sospettoso*. But the fatal shipwreck of the Great Armada produced irreparable confusion in the Spanish people, for, believing that they were the chosen people, they had to ask themselves: 'Why does this disaster come upon us? *Si Dominus nobiscum est, ubi sunt mirabilia ejus?*' Thus a deep depression fell upon all with fatal results thereafter. And so among all the causes of the decline of the Spanish Empire which have been so carefully studied and discussed, history must set as the very first and principal one the abandonment of Isabel's selective system, so clearly shown in the case of Medinasidonia.

The high qualities of Philip II and the greatness of his political vision kept the Empire in the crescent stage, but it was evident that the wane would soon follow. The Book of Capabilities, which was the symbol of efficient government, was given up by Philip III, or rather by his favourite. Bermudez de Pedraza in 1620, when noting great injustice in the allotment of privileges, misses the register book in the office of the royal secretaries. That is to say, when the decline began to be clear to all, simultaneously the desire for a selective system had ceased to exist. Henceforth it is not the most suitable candidate who will receive the post but the one who is the luckiest office-seeker. The evolution is absolutely clear. The Catholic kings created and organized for the first time a complete training-school for candidates for office, and they spread their net far and wide throughout their kingdom. Charles V continued this system of selecting, grouping and encouraging the best men for service. Philip II inherited this rich legacy of human talent, but at times he employed men of no account, and when he did make use of the many illustrious personalities around him he cut their wings and refused to allow them any initiative, for he was suspicious of what they would do in their hour of triumph. Philip III, unintelligent and apathetic, drove away the select men and chose as his favourite one of inferior capacity, and through him lost, as Quevedo says, the inheritance of doughty men which his father had bequeathed to him, wherefore the whole government crumbled away.

When the forceful government of the Prudent King ceased there followed an uncontrollable burst of envious plotting. After Philip III had been reigning seven years, the Venetian ambassador Simon Contarini, when describing the Spanish court, observes that there is no rivalry for public office, but only for private gain, and he ends: 'There is nought here save prejudice and passion; no nation suffers more from mutual jealousy.' Once more envy is the order of the day and there is complete lack of selective efficiency. It is the period of Rodrigo Calderón, when office-selling was rampant. Contarini himself notes that the favourite, the Duke of Lerma, accepts bribes and keeps far from the Court the best brains of Spain. This judgement itself is a full explanation of the decline, and it coincides with that of Quevedo and is confirmed by the evidence which Pinheiro da Veiga, resident in Valladolid, gathered here and there from various sources during those years. He says: 'The Duke of Medinasidonia is to be appointed commander of the fleet; he will do with it what he did with our expedition to England (in effect Medinasidonia repeated his mishaps in his new command); and another who has never seen the sea nor India is to be named Viceroy there; and others who have never seen action are to be made members of the War Council. They believe that to be a count, marquis, or grandee is to be omniscient. . . . Empires were successful as long as they went in search of men and brought them in from the deserts to govern. If this were the method used in Spain there would be no lack of men to fill the posts nor would so many be forgotten.' As time went on the lack of selectivity increased, the downward slope became steeper. How complete it was under Philip IV we know from the striking records of Don Juan Palafox y Mendoza[1] who relates how he saw everywhere '*tantos hombres sin emplear, tantos empleos sin hombres*' (so many men without posts, so many posts without men). These lines do but condense in concise form the thoughts contained in the words of Pinheiro da Veiga quoted above, which refer to the reign of Philip III.

[1] Juan de Palafox y Mendoza (1600–1659), a writer of many historical and religious works, was Bishop of Puebla de los Angeles in Mexico.

THE HISTORICAL CONCEPT OF SELECTION
AND ENVY

In forming a general concept of the history of Spain the depression reached under the Austrian monarchy has been taken as the main viewpoint, and, as we shall see, there are authors who believe that characteristics similar to those of that decline are visible before and after the Austrian period. One should then speak not of a decline, but of a congenital infirmity which has always menaced the Spanish people. This comparison with human pathology, like all similes, can both clarify and confuse at the same time. Applying it to the subject before us, instead of saying that Spain irreparably lacks something possessed by all peoples of normal health, we should say that Spain is, among the great peoples who have played a part in history, the one where selectivity is exercised with the greatest difficulty. Enviousness, together with the isolation in which Spain tends to live, will not allow her to see in the unity of other nations the qualities necessary for success. The power of selection is blunted by the egoism of individuals and groups. The difficulty does not lie in the qualities of the mass of the people, but in the ruling minorities, for to them and not to the mass belong the subtle tasks of selection. It is a defect of the minority and for this reason less constant in its effects.

No doubt the periods of depression due to faults of selection occur much too frequently in Spanish history. But they are not continuous, and it must be the historian's special care to bring into relief those intervals when justice and efficient selection were the rule, in other words, the periods of prosperity both political and social. An examination of these, pointing out the effects of the special individualism we have been discussing, should take the place of the uniform notion of congenital deficiency. Alternations of selective prosperity, such as reached its height under Charles III, and complete depreciation of human values, such as touched its lowest depths under Ferdinand VII, are constantly repeated in Spanish history, though not always in such violent contrast. But no inquiry into the causes, based on documentary evidence, has been made; nor has use been made, for historical purposes, of the great writers, from Feijóo to Larra, who most concerned themselves with problems arising from this lack of selection. As regards cultural life, though similar alternations of abundance and scarcity in first rate men is evident, again there is no study of the causes of these fluctuations, which do not coincide with those of political life. The highpoints of literary and artistic life—the most complex product of periods of selection—generally occur at the end of such periods and the beginning of periods of political and social decline.

The simile we quoted concerning the congenital infirmity of the Spanish people has foundations of fact in the notorious disproportion we can observe between the rise and fall in these alternations. The depression may appear to continue without a break, for its predominance is natural. Selection needs constant care in order that full profit may be drawn from the free development of any talent possessed by the individual; care also is needed in order to guess who will be the unknown hero; and care, too, is necessary if only to save the tender bud that will produce the flower that men desire. Every inferior being called upon to rule over any aspect of the life of a community easily and necessarily enters into relationship with other inferior beings, who are always in the majority, and he finds himself immediately surrounded by a powerful group. The oil stain in each negative selection spreads with far greater rapidity than in the case of a positive one. Gradually the best men find fewer points of support in other select people, for the disorganization of society secludes these and sets them aside instead of grouping them together and strengthening them: 'Where the blind lead the way, woe to those who come behind.' This being so, the gradual disappearance of vigour, intellect and virtue in a period of decline is not always due to the degeneration of the mass of the people which produces too few talented individuals, but to lack of judgement in the ruling classes, because the failure to make adequate selection repels the most talented and renders them useless. Certainly if the action of envy and the consequent weakening of the best elements continues for a long time there is bound to be a decline in the number of births of well-endowed individuals. But the contrary is also true, that selection causes an increase of vitality, and the persistence of selective action may even bring into predominance as a majority a type different to the one which had always prevailed when matters ran their own way and there was no selection.

Just as we noticed in the case of the alternation between justice and arbitrariness, so on this other alternative between selection and envy (a mere variant of the former) is based all the mechanism of rise and decline, and it is this mechanism which can explain the heights and depressions of our vital curve better than the other themes which generally absorb the attention of historians. It is not necessary to devote attention to the well-intentioned programmes drawn up after 1898, to the undertakings which range from urgent national reconstruction to grandiose plans for the future. All that is important is to see whether behind these attempts there is an efficient, just and selective action, or whether time is being wasted in attending merely to unconditional supporters at a moment when the country, which is passing through a lean period, cannot, even with all its resources, manage to carry out its functions with regularity. We have shown as a remarkable example how great results were achieved in a short period of time by the tenacious work of Isabel and Ferdinand. Spaniards of different ideologies often look back to the period of the Catholic monarchs with longing regret as an incomparable epoch, unique in Spanish history, a golden age that the nation enjoyed through some inexplicable design of Providence. We have indicated that the primary explanation of this success is the perfect system of selection adopted by those monarchs, and we consider this is a suggestive case to set against the opposite conception of congenital deficiency. A similar selective policy has brought at other moments in the past and may bring in the future, the same blossoming forth of full collective capacity, and it is of secondary importance, in the study of causes, whether the historical scene on which this total capacity develops is of greater or smaller dimensions.

WAS THERE A LACK OF SELECT MINORITIES?

The short duration of the selective moments in modern Spain makes the depression in its historical curve seem continuous, and causes the belief that there is a permanent congenital defect which authorities from Costa and Macías Picavea[1] onwards

---

[1] Ricardo Macías Picavea (1847–1899), novelist and sociologist, and one of the early writers to reflect the deep political anxiety in the future of Spain in his work *El Problema Nacional*, 1891.

attribute to the lack of an *élite*, a chosen minority who could direct the life of the country. In Spain, it is said, everything is done by the people; the people, deprived of a ruling minority, without any pre-established plan; the strong individualism rooted in the mass of the people brings with it the pride of the inferior who will not allow himself to be directed by his superior. It is certainly true that many Spanish activities whether in the political or the cultural sphere have a special mark which is called popular, but as this designation lends itself to a false interpretation, it should be avoided or at least explained.

The people as a mere collective mass, without any guidance, is incapable of taking any initiative. We cannot to-day continue to believe in the romantic theory that the people is the author of many things such as the four lines of a folk poem, the notes of the simplest melody, the drafting of a law or a treaty: all these are never the work of the people but of an individual, a chosen one, who emerges from the common herd. Even the most primitive manifestation of the folk cannot be produced without the leavening of a minority.

What can be said is that the Spanish people does not necessarily lack leading minorities but that those minorities have peculiar characteristics of their own which cause their actions to appear ineffective, even null and void. Spanish aristocracy, both that of talents and that of social position, does not aspire to the position of a class apart, above the level of the common herd, nor does it aspire to carry out eventually a personal policy of its own within a small minority group; rather does it devote all its activities to the majority: thus it adopts a style of unaffected simplicity based upon broad human values. This does not mean that a work which is directed to the majority of the citizens may not be select, profound and suggestive. Cervantes wrote *Don Quixote* to be read by the entire Spanish people, high and low; surely nobody will place him second when such a masterpiece is compared with another excellent work, the '*Soledades*' of Góngora, which was written for a small coterie of men of letters.

When a leader wishes to create a work for the general majority he does not claim absolute authority to the exclusion of all others. He does not even neglect the co-operation of those he leads, for he recognizes that the latter may possess greater powers of initiative than he has. According to the Spanish legend, the

Cid ordered his troops not to break their ranks, but when Pedro Bermudez did break them, the Cid helped him and backed up the wild initiative which led to victory. In the Roman legend Manlius Torquatus, when his son returned triumphant from single combat, ordered him to be beheaded because he had broken ranks contrary to the commands of his father. Such harshness is repugnant to a Spaniard. Pulgar in his book '*Claros Varones*' justifies it only by saying that the Romans must have been very undisciplined when they needed to have such a cruel example before them.

In any work destined to sway majorities, in addition to this sharing of leadership which counts on the help of the directed, we find also a fragmentation of leadership among a large number of directors. This is very characteristic of Spanish individualism which often tends to split up into little operative groups. When we consider the conduct of war, which most rigorously calls for command, Spain has given us as a model two special types—the guerrilla fighter and the conquistador. Both represent the organization created by the individual against an enemy far superior in numbers. The guerrilla fighter is engaged against armies that are superior in resources and technique; the conquistador against an enemy superior in numbers but inferior in arms. The guerrilla fighters became famous when the Peninsula was invaded by the troops of Napoleon and the name guerrilla spread through Europe and was used in various languages to describe the tactics employed by other countries when they found themselves in a situation resembling the Spanish War of Independence. The conquistador, on the other hand, has remained a peculiarity of Spain, for neither English nor Dutch colonists evolved this special type which implies the diffuse collaboration of the whole nation in a work of expansion and civilization. While the colonization of Anglo-Saxon America was the work of commercial companies and Puritan expatriates, namely small groups which sought wellnigh uninhabited lands where they might carry on their industry and serve God according to their own consciences, the colonization of Hispano-America was a genuinely national work at the service of God and King, propagating the Gospel to a number of primitive peoples and incorporating them in the millenary culture of Europe.

Spanish colonization is the best model for minorities who exercise powers of direction which will call majorities into action. The religious-cultural design was initially conceived by Isabel even before the discovery of the New World was completed. To this plan which was of the highest universalist idealism was added afterwards the contribution of the jurists and theologians who were considered the greatest in Europe. With them collaborated high administrative and commercial enterprises such as the Council of the Indies and the *Casa de Contratación* (Board of Trade). Finally the work was carried out by a host of conquistadores and explorers among whom such men as Balboa, Magellan, Elcano and Orellana, investigators of the geographical secrets of the planet, may well figure, though belonging to a different sphere of human activities, beside the great investigators of the universe such as Copernicus, Tycho Brahe or Kepler.

There is no other nation which can show similar collective movements that should be called, not popular, but national. The people produced its guerrilla fighters and conquistadores because, in spite of its individualism, it was capable of becoming inspired by great collective ideals. The full national scope of its reactions is often not appreciated, but even in cases where such movements appear to be amorphous we may recognize in them a superior guiding inspiration. The Gaul Trogus Pompeius, who is always a valuable starting-point for the observation of Hispanic traits, judges adversely, as devoid of high direction, the anti-Roman resistance in the Iberian Peninsula, and notes that during the various centuries of struggle, the Spaniards had only one great commander, Viriathus. But to this we should add that the Gauls themselves had only one, less of a strategist and less victorious, Vercingetorix, and when he fell all his people were conquered; whilst the Spaniards, before and after Viriathus, prolonged the war for 200 years under the leadership of many chiefs who were anonymous or quasi-anonymous. Their weakness was more than anything else due to their lack of cohesion, but they maintained for two centuries the spirit of national independence, a thing that no other province of the Roman Empire did. Certainly the Iberian guerrillas had no ideological organization as the conquistadores and explorers had later, but they had no lack of patriotism, and this spirit gave to their fragmentary actions a certain vague unity which could always become effective at determined moments. In periods that are better documented we find that the resistance during the 300 most difficult years when weak Christian Spain faced the far superior power of Islam, although it was diffuse and languid in its direction, yet counted many kings and captains, who far from being anonymous, enjoyed illustrious fame, such as Pelayo,[1] Alfonso the Catholic, Sancho Abarca, Fernán González, Ramiro II, Vifredo el Velloso, all of whom symbolize the collective consciousness of duty towards universal Christianity. In the centuries following the Reconquest we find examples of a diffuse and chaotic frontier activity, but already there begins the predominance of great kings and heroes, conquistadores and campeadores, all agreeing in pacts whereby they shared their efforts against Islam and co-operated one with the other in times of difficulty.

MAJORITIES AND MINORITIES

In all historical epochs there is certainly no lack of excellent leaders of the masses. What often is lacking, however, is agreement among them, and the efficient daily co-ordination of effort which unites the wills of all, thus ensuring the greatest benefit. Minorities, both those of capacity and those of command, organize themselves only with great difficulty and do not usually show the generous cohesion, the selective justice and the other virtues of leadership, and by allowing the vice of envy to run riot in their hearts they destroy any chances of success. The contrary takes place in the common run of people where the individual often gives proof of positive virtues. The most salient of all is the keen sense of personal dignity which lends lustre to a man's whole life. We can perceive this quality even in the poorest classes, in the most humiliating situations, and this fact has been noted by all foreign observers from Lucius Marineus Siculus[2] onwards. Spanish literature has celebrated this virtue in many a noble

---

[1] Pelayo, first king of Asturias in the eighth century; the other personalities mentioned are the primitive kings and counts of Asturias, Navarre, León, Castile and Catalonia.

[2] Lucio Marineo Siculo (1460?–1533?), Sicilian humanist, settled in Spain 1484 as tutor to the young nobles. Wrote *De rebus Hispaniae memorabilibus*, 1530, *Epistolarum libri decem et septem*, 1914.

poem, and it has also satirized the excesses due to its deep influence. Above all, literature has dramatized the impulse that causes a man to defend his personal dignity when it has been injured. When this concept of honour is examined in its most typical literary expression we find that even Menéndez Pelayo and Unamuno, who possessed such deep understanding of the national character, considered it not as a virtue, as we have presented it here, but as a disordered and unhealthy pride, a peevish fear of public opinion, productive of deeply immoral tragedies as a solution. But this is to misrepresent a certain poetic stylization (very Spanish indeed in its exaggeration), taking it as the normal or fundamental form. The most implacable and monstrous vindications of the offences against honour that have been the theme of Spanish literature sprang from the individual considering himself as the trustee and the responsible champion of the essential values in collective life. Individual honour is one part of the social structure of the entire community and the tragedies which it inspires represent a point of contact between the individual and consciousness of social solidarity. But these tragedies are not, as has always been believed, a morbid exaggeration of passion peculiar to the Spanish baroque epoch. On another occasion I have examined mediaeval subjects quite as Calderonian as those of Calderón and I was able to prove that the exalted passion for honour must be set among the enduring characteristics of Spain. We must here add that the jealous sentiment of honour has not been dramatized in the Spanish theatre merely with reference to the class of the nobility, as other literatures have done, but it has also been represented as the element giving dignity to the plebeian and rustic class of the Spanish nation in the seventeenth century. We may finally conclude that in contrast to eminent minorities, the gregarious majority possesses to a greater degree the good qualities of its class, and exercises them even when its leaders are found wanting. It is strange to note that when Quevedo in 1609 considered that all the virtues that shone in a Cisneros, a Cortés, and in those who created the greatness of the nation were extinguished, he nevertheless praised the Spanish people for preserving intact their virtues, their discipline, their loyalty to their princes, their religious obedience to the laws, their love for their generals and captains to the generous disregard for their own lives. At a very different period we find this trait noted by Vittorio Alfieri who travelled through Spain in 1771. He considered that the Spanish and the Portuguese peoples were the only ones in Europe who preserved their customs intact, and although their high exploits always failed owing to their innumerable blunders (that is to say, owing to the mistakes of the group that rules), yet he believed that both peoples possessed the raw material for carrying out great enterprises, especially military ones, for they were gifted to a high degree with all the necessary qualities, namely, valour, perseverance, honour, moderation, obedience, patience, and high mindedness. This comparison between minorities and majorities is repeated many times by modern observers.

And so, far from putting down the weakness of Spain to the indocile nature of the people which is unable to follow the lead of its select minority, we must attribute it to the discord and want of harmony existing among the members of that select minority, to their deficiencies which split up and disperse all sense of leadership and direction. The war against Napoleon was the most remarkable example of this. Spain, abandoned by all her leaders, then displayed the most spontaneous national spirit of unity and firmly struck out for her independence, even though she was divided under fragmentary leadership, and in addition torn within by two opposing ideologies.

In conclusion Spanish individualism can harmonize with high collective ideals, and when this is the case, the people, the majority, produces in great profusion its ruling minorities. Castile exercises hegemony over her brother peoples in the Peninsula, because in individualistic Spain, Castile preserves in its popular masses a more efficient individualism. The Catholic King considered what he called *desconcierto* or predominance of the individual an essential element in the life of Castile and one which differentiated it from Aragon. And Castile with its predominance of the individual was able to furnish this loose leadership, characteristic of the majority movements which are so much in keeping with the nature of all the Hispanic peoples.

Chapter IV

Centralization and Regionalism

The individualism felt by a whole region, that is to say local individualism as an obstacle against fully concerted action between various regions, has predominated to such an extent on occasions that it lends itself to erroneous interpretation historically when localism is considered the essential and absolute element in the life of the Spanish people. Once again we find ourselves inclining to consider as unique one of the two active opposing tendencies. Both tendencies we shall treat when we come to explain the various historical periods. Here, nevertheless, we shall proceed to show that the centralizing tendency was always in the ascendant, at one moment as the only vital force in periods of increase and prosperity, at another having at its side as an inferior force the localist sentiment in periods of decline.

EXCESS OF LOCALISM

It is clear that there is in Spain an especial weakness in the spirit of association. The benefits to be derived from co-operation are less clearly felt than the advantages of separate individual action, even though this, in the long run, shows less results. Communal life comes to be regarded as something hampering owing to the restrictions it imposes upon the individual, for every one wishes to work at his ease without having to take account of his neighbour. This weakens the relationship between the different provinces as has been noted at various periods by foreign observers. A French traveller, Bartolomé Joly, was surprised in 1604 at the localism prevalent in the minds of Aragonese, Valencians, Catalans, Biscayans, Galicians, and Portuguese, for their habitual entertainment was to tell one another their defects, and he even found that those from Old Castile felt contempt for those from New Castile. The same observation was made by Richard Ford half-way through the nineteenth century; he encountered in Spain a shy and diffident local spirit, where the link between the peasantry was even more exclusive than among the Irish of Tipperary or the Scots. Théophile Gautier, when he heard in the Puerta del Sol descriptions of certain atrocities of the Carlist War related with complete indifference, and the reason given for this indifference being that 'the incident happened in Old Castile and there was no need to worry about it,' finds in this answer the summary of the contemporary Spanish situation and the key to many things that had appeared incomprehensible when seen from France.

But it is not so easy to interpret the localist spirit. The Spaniard who visits the great cities of America is astonished to find that the Spanish colony have built a magnificent Club, be it Galician, Asturian, Riojan or Catalan, but not one all-including Spanish Club. It is easy to draw the conclusion that the higher concept of one Spain is lacking, but in reality what has happened is that those Spanish emigrants do not feel foreign in the New Spain which they inhabit, nor do they feel inclined to evoke their fatherland, and so they find that the most immediate and intimate method of expressing their love for old Spain is to concentrate all their patriotism on their particular locality. Nevertheless love for one's homeland which is bound up with the unfading recollections of infancy remains a mean and poor thing if experience and the generous ideas of youth do not enlarge it so as to include the Fatherland itself; just as patriotism degenerates and becomes a limitation to man's spirit if his greater maturity does not lead him to share it with the universal fatherland, namely with every other country from which he receives some beneficial inspiration towards a higher life, and it cannot be denied that the Spaniard allows his local patriotism to prevail excessively. The fact of having been born in the same province creates among Spaniards a sense of companionship and an obligation to help one another which is as great as or even greater than that among relatives, and this causes them to become rigidly exclusive in their dealings with others.

This local particularism, as Théophile Gautier said, explains a good part of Spanish history, and there are authors like Martin Hume, in his History of the Spanish People, who continually insist upon this characteristic, both in its causes and in its effects. According to Hume, regionalism is due to ethnological variety which is maintained by the mountainous nature of the country. Spain in fact is, owing to its geography, a country of divisions, for its enormous mountain barriers separate one province from another. In this soil the basis is represented by the Iberians, brothers of the Berbers, two peoples equally individualistic. Afterwards came the Celts, Afro-Semites, Carthaginians, Greeks, Romans, French, Goths, and the mixed hordes of Islam, leaving relics of population hidden away in the countless valleys of the Peninsula. Adopting the same geographical method Herculano explained the formation of the mediaeval kingdoms as due to the difficulty of communication across the high mountains, but not even the lofty mountains have as much decisive power to isolate as is attributed to them, nor in Spain do they limit the regions which were most influenced by the spirit of autonomy. The great mountains that run from north to south of Catalonia are very much towards the east of the country but not on the boundary with Aragon; the hundred tunnels of the northern railway do not separate Castile from León, but León from Asturias; the Portuguese frontier, too, is not decided by mountain ranges. And with regard to the racial question, apart from the fact that the so-called brotherhood of Iberians and Berbers is untenable in view of the radical differences of language existing between one and the other, and the similar divergence of abilities, the dissimilarity of races in the Peninsula is not perceptibly greater than that existing, for instance, in France. The greater localism of Spain does not depend upon a multitude of ethnico-geographical reasons, but on the contrary, on a uniform psychological condition; it depends upon the original exclusive character of the Iberians, already noted by the authors of antiquity long before there came to the Peninsula even the half of the races enumerated by Hume as causing the dispersive tendencies. The fact that the ethnico-geographical characteristics of the Peninsula do not imply any special tendency towards splitting up into fragments is shown by the variety of dialects in Spain which is much less than that of France or Italy.

Also it is incorrect to hold that local sentiment was so strong and deep-seated that it was able to prevent the creation of all national Spanish feeling up to recent times. It is commonly held that this idea of one Spain only began to grow up in modern times, an opinion which apparently derives from the widely-read prologue which Lafuente wrote for his History. When speaking of the title chosen by the successors of the Catholic monarchs, he writes: 'King of Spain, a term long-wished for but one which we were not able to pronounce in all the centuries of history we have traversed up to this point'. Lafuente speaks only of the royal title, but not even in this limited sense is his observation correct, for he forgets that the title *Hispaniae rex* was used in the eleventh and twelfth centuries not only within the Peninsula, but outside, even by the great international power of those days, the Roman Curia.

THE CONCEPT OF SPAIN IN ANTIQUITY

In the first century B.C. Strabo made observations concerning Spanish individualism similar to those made by modern writers. He noted that the Iberians possessed greater local pride than the Greeks and this prevented them from uniting together in a powerful confederation. If they had been able to link together their forces, the greater part of Iberia would not have been subdued by Carthaginians, Celts and Romans. Thus Strabo, while noting the weakness of collective spirit in the Iberians, yet recognizes its existence as a factor in assuring the independence of the Iberian community. Livy on his side considers *Hispania* as an entity and speaks frequently of the *Hispani* in general, without deeming it necessary to state whether they come from this or that tribe. Later Florus, an African historian who lived at Tarragona, uses the very expressive phrase *Hispania universa* to describe a human collectivity and like Strabo blames Spain for not recognizing its own strength until it had been conquered by Rome after a struggle lasting 200 years. He thus implies a common interest neglected, a nation with an imperfect sense of nationality.

Within the Roman administrative organization Spain, though divided into various provinces, was always considered as a higher entity uniting the provincial divisions. And under the splendour of the Empire, when for the first time we can observe the full cultural development of Romanized Spain, we note that it forms a unity similar in its distribution of forces and values to what modern Spain became at another Imperial moment, namely in the time of its greatest unity during the golden ages of its literature. So too in antiquity the central part of the country, as afterwards Castile, represented the cohesive nucleus, *Celtiberia robur Hispaniae*. Then, too, this Celtiberian centre, together with Baetica, produced all the great representative men in letters and in politics, just as in the sixteenth and seventeenth centuries the greatest number of them came from Aragon, the two Castiles and Andalusia. The similarity between the 'intellectual map' (as Feijóo would say) of Roman Spain and Austrian Spain is surprising: and such similarity between the two most brilliant moments of unified Spain shows that this spiritual unity was governed by certain organic principles, by certain vital energies which endured in action and in strength.

Roman Spain, shortly before the dissolution of the Empire, appeared already with a precise national significance in the first Universal History composed by a Christian, that of Paulus Orosius.[1] This Galician disciple of Saint Augustine possessed to a special degree the sense of patriotism. Spain for him was still a province of the Empire within which Divine Providence had unified the world, but, in spite of this, the Province rises proudly in opposition to the City, affirming an historical destiny of its own, within the Empire, and claiming for the wars it had waged against Rome greater accord with the eternal laws of justice than that shown by the conquering metropolis. Orosius pointed to the Goths in Spain as the people ready to play a part which would restore the providential unity of the Christian world.

GOTHIC UNITY AND ITS DESTRUCTION

Immediately after Orosius, the Roman Empire of the west was dismembered into various Germanic Kingdoms. An important factor in the strengthening of the weakening unity of the Iberian people was the fact that at the time of the invasions the

---

[1] Paulo Orosio, native of Bracara, to-day Braga, travelled to Africa and Palestine, visited S. Augustine at Hippo in 414 and 416 and S. Jerome in Bethlehem in 415. He wrote the first universal history of Christianity. His work *Historiarum adversus paganos libri septem* was written in the years 416–417.

last emperors handed over the pacification of Spain to the Visi-goths, who were the most Romanized of the Germans, entirely convinced that the Roman idea of the State as the arbiter of good and justice for the whole community was one that was superior to the dominant particularism of the rest of the barbarian govern-ments. Those Goths, although they were Arians and conse-quently adverse to the Catholicism of the Hispano-Romans, yet unified politically the entire peninsula, and some years later unified it spiritually by becoming converted to Catholicism. The strength of national sentiment which the Gothic unification aroused even in the period of the heterodox monarchs may be seen in the case of the rebellion of Saint Hermenegildo against his Arian father which was censured even by the Catholic clergy that had to suffer persecution at the hands of the public authori-ties. This national sentiment achieves enthusiastic literary expression in the writings of Saint Isidore: over all the wide world, from its oriental boundaries in India to the extreme west, holy Mother Spain is the fairest and happiest land, incomparable in its natural riches, the fatherland of famous princes. After a first union with the conquering fortress of Romulus, she has now celebrated a new betrothal with the glorious and flourishing nation of the Goths.

The idea of a united Roman-Gothic Spain which was so nobly portrayed by Orosius, and so eloquently exalted by Saint Isidore, never ceased to be present to the spirits of men during the following centuries, for both those authors were widely read all through the Middle Ages. Nevertheless, this idea did become obscured. After the prosperous period of Leovigildo[1] and Saint Isidore, the Gothic Kingdom declined into an anarchical contest between different parties, and the party struggle obscured national sentiment. One of the parties called to its help the Mos-lems and when these turned from allies to invaders all possibility of cohesion and unity in the face of national danger faded away. The result was chaos and every man for himself. The sons of Vitiza[2] contented themselves with retaining possession of their 3,000 patrimonial estates under a guarantee from the invaders;

[1] Leovigildo reigned between 573–586 and brought the Gothic kingdom to its highest power and political unity. He was the last Arian king. In 579–584 his, eldest son Hermenegildo, on being converted to Catholicism, rebelled against him, but was defeated and killed in prison, 585.

[2] Penultimate Gothic king of Spain, 702–708.

Teodomir secured another special pact at Orihuela; various principal lords cleverly managed to preserve their property, their religion and their laws and paid no attention to the rest of the country. As late as in the eleventh century an Aragonese lord boasted that he as well as his ancestors had lived independent of the caliphs of Córdoba and the Kings of Aragon, *quia libertas nostra antiqua est*. When Spain was faced with ruin, these powerful barons, saturated with individualism, had no other thought in life but to preserve unimpaired their utmost freedom. The characteristic Iberian unsociability had broken out everywhere like a plague, which, when strength diminishes, invades the whole body. One centre of resistance organized itself to carry on the combat, namely Asturias, but it fought on weakly in isolation. Nobody was interested in the plight of his neighbour. The Mozarab in Toledo who, full of sorrow, wrote an extensive chronicle for the year 754 does not say a word about Pelayo or Alfonso I; perhaps he did not even know about them or he did not consider their audacious wars and raids of importance.

THE MEDIAEVAL KINGDOMS

Thus began a long period of disintegration, truly a long one, because the formation of many new states on the ruins of the Visigothic Kingdom was favoured by the tendency to disintegration brought by the feudal epoch to all Europe. We should note, however, that Iberian individualism did not organize itself within the régime of vassalage which was the basis of feudalism, but in the form of independent kingdoms. By the side of the primitive Asturian-Neogothic kingdom there rose the kingdom of Pamplona in 905, the kingdoms of Castile and Aragon in 1035 and that of Portugal in 1143. The ancient Astur-Leonese kingdom possessed over the others a vague, though significant imperial superiority, a weak Spanish substitute for the equally weak bond of vassalage which linked up the European feudal system.

It has been pointed out as a great misfortune for Spain that it never had feudalism, that is to say, a strong, enterprising nobility. But if it did not have a number of feudal states, it had a variety of kingdoms which were able in a freer way to develop their personality and spread their influence far and wide through the Mediterranean, through Africa and the Atlantic, as an apprenticeship and trial for the greatness achieved when those kingdoms became reunited in the sixteenth century. There were no powerful barons, but there were a number of kings at the same time, who directed in rivalry enterprises of a kind that no feudal duke could ever have dreamt of. The division into kingdoms retarded the main enterprise, the Reconquest, but in exchange it caused the various expansive actions outside the Peninsula. Among the Islamized Spaniards the Taifa Kingdoms of the eleventh to the thirteenth centuries show development similar to that of the five Christian Kingdoms. Just as the latter were in opposition to European feudalism, so the Taifa kings, even to a greater degree, fought against the spirit of Islam, both by their tributary system and by their regarding the kingdom as their personal property to be divided among their heirs, as did the Christians of the north. Thus Spain, as always, was in disagreement with the two worlds that crossed one another's path on her soil. At the fall of the Caliphate of Córdoba the Islamized Iberianism caused the creation of more than twenty little kingdoms, which later were reduced to a smaller number owing to successive reincorporations. In vain the great African empires of the Almorávides and the Almóhades crossed in turn the Straits and reimposed Islam in El Andalús and re-established political unity there. As soon as the African invasions lost their impetus, then inevitably the Taifa kingdoms rose again.

And when we follow the parallel between Christian and Islamic disintegration we must likewise admit as regards the Taifa kingdoms a certain advantage, while recognizing the great weakness which the division of territory brought to Moslem power. Each petty king wished to surpass his neighbour by reason of the plentiful library which he had managed to gather together, or the number of distinguished poets and men of science he had been able to attract to his court. Thanks to this many-sided impulse Spanish Islam produced a brilliant cultural display before its extinction. Shortly before Jaime I and Saint Ferdinand destroyed these Moorish seigniories, the benefits of this disintegration were celebrated in the 'Eulogy of Spanish Islam' which was written by El Secundi[1] about 1200 in praise of the magnificence

[1] El Secundi, Andalusian-Arab, man of letters, died in 1231. He was called Secundi from his birthplace Secunda, a small Roman village situated opposite Córdoba on the left bank of the Guadalquivir.

of the ancient petty kingdoms of Seville, Almería, Toledo, Valencia and Denia. 'All the kings of the Taifas,' he says, 'rivalled one another in their longing for culture: every day was for them a feast and they gathered round them all branches of knowledge.' And this cultural rivalry was of transcendental importance, for it was by absorbing and utilizing the science created by these Moorish kingdoms for centuries that Alfonso X merited the epithet of 'the Learned' in Western Christendom.

THE IDEA OF SPAIN IN THE MIDDLE AGES

But the destruction of the Gothic kingdom, followed by the long-drawn out period of disintegration, did not blot out of men's minds the idea of unity, but only obscured it. It banished the idea from political life, but not from men's aspirations. For the mediaeval kingdoms never broke Gothic unity in an arbitrary manner but tried to patch it up and save it from destruction. They came into being naturally and spontaneously as guerrilla fighters of Iberian individualism, who began the struggle against the Islam colossus when it was at its zenith of power. These kingdoms served no local patriotism. Localism has as its chief basis a linguistic difference, but none of those kingdoms, except that of Portugal, founded its power upon a language basis. León, Castilla, Navarra and Aragon were all bilingual. All sprang into being as a first step towards reintegration, the only one possible in view of the superior power of the Moslem. For this reason the long existence of these kingdoms did not blot out the idea of Hispanic unity which remained stronger than the temporary division.

Very soon after the Moslem invasion, the Asturian kings proclaimed themselves kinsmen and heirs to the Gothic kings. In 883 Alfonso III, when writing the first history of the small kingdom of Oviedo, calls it the History of the Goths, proclaiming by this title the uninterrupted continuity of the Gothic monarchy and declaring expressly that the small kingdom of Pelayo was the salvation of Spain, *salus Hispaniae*, for it would not cease to fight 'day and night until divine predestination decreed the total expulsion of the Saracens'. It is noteworthy that the Kingdom of Asturias, in spite of its insignificant size, insisted that the soil of Spain should not be divided among the Christians of old and the

Moorish invaders, though this seemed the likely course, considering the overwhelming power of the Caliphates of Damascus and Córdoba; and in view of the relative strengths of the two antagonists, such an enterprise did actually entail many centuries of struggle. Asturias would not be contented with less than the firm determination that Islam should not remain installed in Spain in perpetuity. Thus the Moslem invasion, instead of achieving its purpose whereby the small Christian territories of the north, feeling themselves estranged from the rest of Spain which was solidly Islamized, would abandon the old concept of Saint Isidore, actually strengthened that concept by inspiring the northern kingdoms with a religious ideal as well as with the patriotic resolve to recover the national territory. This political idea by the very fact that it was of immense difficulty and of slow achievement, was a deeply formative one, and influenced men through centuries. The fact that this idea of total reconquest was conceived and expressed as an Hispanic idea shows that there was a very deeply-rooted national feeling in the country. No similar idea was conceived or attempted by any of the other provinces of the ancient Roman Empire in the west or the west which had fallen as a prey to the Moslems; with the exception of Spain not one of them reacted, when Islam began the gigantic struggle against Christendom for the domination of the world.

Asturias thus served as initiator and teacher in this ideal of resistance and total restoration, which, as centuries passed, became less disproportionate and unattainable. The various kingdoms which rose later all proclaimed the same resolve which implied unity of origin and destiny. All recognized in the total re-conquest a *united Hispanic enterprise*, and by means of special treaties they fixed the districts which each one of them had to conquer, or else they all made alliances in order to beat back fresh invasions from Africa, even though those invasions only threatened one of the kingdoms, Castile. Secondly, the various kingdoms also recognized up to the twelfth century a certain *political unity* as the heirs to the Asturian Gothic kings whereby the kings of León took the title of Emperor, or to be more explicit, Emperor of all Spain, *Imperator totius Hispaniae*, and as such they were recognized by the King of Navarre, the King of Aragon, the Count of Barcelona and by many of the Taifa kings. The kings of Navarre and Aragon, Sancho Ramírez and Pedro I, rushed to defend the imperial throne of Toledo when Alfonso VI was attacked by the Almorávides. Then, too, the most popular of heroes, the one celebrated in heroic poetry, gave new strength to the neo-Gothic idea of unity, for in the moment of trial when the war effort of the 'Emperor of all Spain' gave way before the invasion of the Almorávides, Roderick de Vivar proposed by his unaided efforts to restore the whole of the Gothic kingdom which had been destroyed about four centuries before. The restoration was longed for by all, and it was said: 'If a Roderick it was who lost Spain, another Roderick will restore it.' This threat, according to Ben Bassam, filled the Moslems with dread, for the total liberation of Spain was no longer a fantastic dream of Spanish faith as it had been two centuries before for the Asturian people. Besides, as a third unifying element, all the kingdoms felt themselves included within a kind of *cultural unity* based upon a long political and religious tradition common to all Roman and Gothic Spain. All, for instance, at the beginning, were ruled according to the Visigothic code, and it was only in the eleventh century that this was supplanted by laws of local custom amongst which we discover likewise close relationships and reciprocal influences between one kingdom and another. Finally, all the kingdoms became every day more closely associated and reached a *dynastic unity*, for from the eleventh century onwards their kings descended from a common stock owing to the frequent matrimonial alliances. And these dynastic relationships, in addition to implying close intimacy in the government of the various kingdoms, were an inspiration to still closer union. The attempt to link Castile and Aragon through the disastrous marriage of Alfonso the Battler[1] was followed by the effective union of Aragon and Barcelona, and later by that of Castile and León, both the result of marriages. Later the 'Compromise of Caspe' meant a

---

[1] Alfonso the Battler, King of Aragon (1104–1134), married the Queen of Castile, Urraca, in 1109; but owing to quarrels between the two the marriage did not result in the political union of Castile and Aragon. The union of Aragon and Barcelona was effected by the marriage of Petronila with Ramon Berenguer IV in 1137. The kingdoms of Castile and León united in the person of Ferdinand III the Saint who inherited both kingdoms owing to the marriage of his mother, Berenguela of Castile, with the King of León, Alfonso IX, in 1197. The Compromise of Caspe in 1412 enthroned in Aragon the Castilian dynasty. The marriage of Ferdinand and Isabel brought about the unity of Aragon and Castile in 1474.

strengthening of dynastic unity. It was through marriage also that the union of Castile and Aragon took place, and the desire for complete unification was rounded off by the various Portuguese marriages which the Catholic monarchs arranged with so great insistence though with such unfortunate results.

The proposal to recover all the soil of the fatherland, which never ceased to appeal to the mass of the people, was felt to have been accomplished in the thirteenth century, and both the people and the kings considered the great work terminated, and were convinced that it had been the united enterprise of all Spain. Among Galician poets and Castilian chroniclers we find a very expressive popular phrase: 'Ferdinand III and Alfonso X won Spain from sea to sea', that is to say from the sea of Asturias to the sea of Seville and Carthagena. Simultaneously James I completed the part of the reconquest that had been entrusted to Aragon, and after this was done, on the occasion of a rising of Moors in Murcia, he rushed to the help of Alfonso X, proclaiming that he and his Catalans wished to win the high renown of *saving Spain*, as the king himself declares in his own chronicle. The total liberation of the fatherland was carried out as a task in common by all the Spaniards.

With the completion of the Reconquest coincides the renaissance of historical studies on Spain, considered as a unity in spite of its division into various kingdoms. In this sense were written the works of the Bishop of Tuy,[1] 'El Tudense', who was a Leonese, and the Archbishop of Toledo, 'El Toledano', who was a Castilianized son of Navarre. Both wrote in the reign of Ferdinand III. The Archbishop of Toledo, Jiménez de Rada, owing to his far greater erudition and his gifts of clarity and style, was more widely read and had greater influence. His work '*De Rebus Hispaniae*' begins by taking as the foundation of Spain's population the government of Tubal and Hercules. It follows the long centuries of unity in Romano-Gothic times and ends with a eulogy of Spain imitating that by Saint Isidore, but followed by what is an important innovation, namely a poetic lament for the destruction of Spain, in which it is announced that its restoration

[1] The History of Lucas, Bishop of Tuy, was finished in 1236. The history *De Rebus Hispaniae* was finished by the Archbishop of Toledo, Jiménez de Rada, in 1243 and the *Estoria de España*, begun by Alfonso X, was finished in the reign of his son, Sancho IV in 1289.

has begun in Asturias and has been continued by the other kingdoms. The dynastic unity of those kingdoms is the basic principle of the second part of the work in which the nucleus is the kingdom of León-Castile.

Within these general lines Alfonso X created his great '*Estoria de España*', a more extensive work than that of El Toledano and richer in narrative. In the prologue he announces as the main theme of his work *the Spaniards* and with a laconic phrase (which is an improvement on the title '*De Rebus Hispaniae*') he says that he is going to relate *El fecho de España* (the Emprise of Spain) and the harm that came to her through being split up into kingdoms (*por partir los regnos*) for it retarded the task of winning back what had been seized by the Moors. But he then adds, '*la ayuntó Dios*', that is to say, God linked together the chief kingdoms. He then goes on to relate how now all the land from the 'sea of Santander to that of Cadiz' has been won, and he ends by relating how Saint Ferdinand left all Spain conquered at his death, and Granada a tributary kingdom which wept for him as its lord and protector. In this way the History culminates in the idea that the Reconquest has been completed. This was virtually the case, though this vassalage of Granada, which satisfied Saint Ferdinand at his death, became for his successors an opiate dulling the concept of their duty, which was to combat Islam. This neglect brought on them the censure of the Aragonese King James II. Finally, we must distinguish above all, in this conception of history, the fact that the division into separate kingdoms was looked upon as a temporary evil which God would remedy. This is an essential political thought necessary to explain the constant tendency towards unification which goes on peacefully through all the later Middle Ages. And this condemnation of separatism and sub-division as being abnormal and harmful was not held by historians and statesmen alone, but by the mass of the people. The 'jongleurs' in their epic songs declaimed against the partition of the kingdoms made by Ferdinand I, saying that the Goths of old made a pact among themselves that never should the Empire of Spain be divided, but that it should all be under one lord. This minstrel poem was of such weight and authority that we find it written in prose in the '*Estoria de España*' itself. Thus in opposition to sporadic localism, the concept of Spanish unity, which was expressed for the first time in the ancient chronicle of Alfonso III, reaches its perfection and highest divulgation in the Latin pages of El Toledano and in the Spanish prose of Alfonso X. These two works served as a guide to all subsequent historians whether from Castile or from Aragon, Navarre or Portugal, and this was the constant reading matter of scholars and masses for five centuries. In spiritual accord with them was every man who felt the inspiration of the past as a spur to the present.

POLITICAL UNITY

The disintegrating period in which five kingdoms were formed finishes with the last partition by inheritance which occurred in 1157. The attempt by Alfonso X to form a kingdom apart with Jaén, destined for the Infante Alfonso de la Cerda, was a temporary expedient which failed as soon as it was made. On the other hand the unifying impulse which had been in operation since the marriage of Ferdinand I and from the wars of Sancho II and the Cid continually asserts itself until final unity is achieved by the Catholic monarchs. The unity which then took place was not an aspiration limited to the upper spheres of the government; it was, we insist, entirely popular. The Aragonese marriage of Isabel in opposition to a foreign marriage was a natural desire of the whole people, and even the children sang of it in their games, as the Parish Priest of Los Palacios, Andrés Bernáldez, tells us.

When political unity was achieved, an attempt was made to secure greater internal unity to the advantage of the central government. Castile was the first, under Charles V, to succumb in its attempt to impose the authority of the Cortes on the King; Aragon followed suit, defending the function of its 'Justiciar' against Philip II. The Renaissance had given to the monarchy a turn which was incompatible with the severe limitations of the Middle Ages. Theorists and ministers continued to combat these traditional limitations in the reigns of Philip III and his son. The Count-Duke Olivares proposed to Philip IV, as the most effective means of making himself a true king of Spain, to reduce the various kingdoms 'to the same style and laws as Castile so that there might be no difference'. But this extremist policy was no longer possible owing to the great decline of the very royalty in whose name it was proposed to unify the various kingdoms, and those apathetic kings were unable to obtain any privileges comparable to those secured by the early Austrian monarchs. On the contrary, local feeling arose as in all periods of great depression. The general decline, the disappearance of the spirit and the ancient virtue which had created the empire, led to very grave secessionist movements all over the country, such as the emancipation of Portugal and the rebellion of Catalonia in addition to two big risings, chaotic affairs but which showed how wide in extent was the evil, that of the Duke of Medinasidonia who was suspected of plotting with Portugal to raise the standard of revolt in Andalusia, relying on the general discontent in that province (1641), and years afterwards a similar attempt by the Duke of Hijar in Aragon, whose adherents, according to Philip IV, seemed to be 'rather madmen than traitors' (1648). In so far as the change of dynasty, at the opening of the eighteenth century, checked the extreme national weakness and brought with it an increase of vitality, the unitary principle was strengthened both in government action and in the ideological sphere.

LOCAL PRIVILEGES
FUEROS, FEUDALISM AND CANTONALISM

The spirit of localism breaks out afresh as an element in the first Carlist war. In this case it is necessary to read the comments of a Catalan writer, Balmes, who in 1843–1847 repeatedly contradicted the opinion which was widely held, especially abroad, that Spain was under the domination of a provincialist spirit, a 'federal spirit', which was opposed to the centralist administration imposed by the monarchy. This is inaccurate, said Balmes: the Spanish people does not cherish federal tendencies opposed to the 'total monarchy' which has been governing and unifying them for three centuries. A proof of this is that all the provinces rose up against Napoleon uttering the cry of 'long live the king' with one accord, spontaneously, without any previous agreement. For this reason it is naïve to believe that the Carlist war was fought in the name of the ancient 'fueros' or charters, for neither the Basques, nor the Catalans, nor the Valencians, nor the Aragonese of to-day know what they signified. Apart from this, the provincialist or federalist movement is upheld and encouraged by some foreign countries that are interested in keeping Spain weak. Starting from these arguments of Balmes we must note that the centrifugal force prevalent in the middle of the nineteenth century cannot claim a traditional link with that which inspired the defenders of Lanuza.[1] It was something fresh and spontaneous that had sprung up as a consequence of the confusion and weakness, both moral and material, which had come upon the country; but there was no doubt that the Carlist monarchy was for unification but not uniformity. The claim for charter rights is an accessory, a parasite on the political and religious principles which the Carlists upheld and which were professed with equal passion by Carlists from regions where there was never any question of demanding special charter privileges. This new tendency, more or less centrifugal, though beaten back when it first appeared, yet reappears at every moment of great national weakness. It is also helped by a far off echo of romantic idealism, springing from the desire of each region that its own special genius should assert and express itself freely and naturally without the interference of the central state. It was in this sense, and as a spokesman for the widest liberalism in politics, that Pí y Margall theorized on the federal principle. Yet, after the revolution of 1868, when the second Carlist war broke out in the north and the Republic was proclaimed, Pí y Margall[2] as president proved how complete was the failure of the federal idea, for he himself had to struggle against the degeneration of that idea into the anarchical cantonalism which broke out in the south of the Peninsula.

NATIONALISM

The reappearance of federalist ideas which has taken place in contemporary times was due to the confusion which arose in Spain after the disaster of 1898. We may add to this an important economic cause, namely, the loss of the colonies which disturbed the commerce of Catalonia and caused serious hardship to that

---

[1] Juan de Lanuza, Chief Justiciar of Aragon, who, basing himself upon the *fueros* or traditional laws and customs of Aragon, tried to resist with arms the decisions of Philip II. He was beheaded in Saragossa on 20 December 1591.

[2] Author of *El principio federativo* (1872) and of *Las Nacionalidades* (1876). He was president of the Federal Republic in 1873 when Malaga, Seville, Cadiz, Carthagena and Valencia rebelled and declared themselves independent cantons.

region. Also the foreign influence to which Balmes referred came to aid the Iberian particularist spirit: the 'small nation politics' which is practised by the big nations for their own benefit; the doctrine of self-determination of countries which has progressed since the first world war.

Catalan federalism among the extremists takes the form of nationalism, and artificially exaggerates the differences which represent the Catalan people, through the course of centuries, as completely and permanently separated from the rest of the Spanish peoples. In order to prove this, History had to be treated from a national standpoint, as was done with great learning by Rovira Virgili[1] among others. But this historical method meets with many difficulties: one has to sever carefully all the strongest ties that link Catalan history and the general history of Spain, and when this is impossible, it is necessary to show how unjust and harmful the ties were. History has to be de-Castilianized. Then we find that the wrongs done to Catalonia do not spring from Philip V or Philip IV but go back to earlier centuries when the dynastic unity of the peninsular kingdoms was strengthened. Thus the Compromise of Caspe, the most famous and exemplary political event of the fifteenth century, is condemned, as though those saintly and learned jurists, who studied and settled the question of succession, were a band of iniquitous judges. Other nationalists go three centuries further back and head the list of historical injustices against Catalonia with Count Raymond Berenguer IV, saying that when he married the Aragonese child-queen he made too many concessions, for he ought to have taken the title of King of Catalonia and Aragon. But those who make this reproach forget one difficulty, namely, that Catalonia then had no clear existence, even in name, for Catalans and Catalonia do not appear in official documents until thirty or forty years later. They also forget that taking the title of king did not depend then, nor afterwards, upon personal whim. Nevertheless, Raymond Berenguer, ignorant of the fact that he would displease the nationalists of the twentieth century, went even further than refusing to call himself king; he actually acknowledged himself to be a vassal of the Emperor of Toledo, Alfonso VII. This fact was published by Zurita, always punctili-

[1] *Historia Nacional de Catalunya*, six volumes, 1922–1931.

ous as an historian, but is omitted by the nationalist Catalan historians, who when they have to speak of the Emperor and the Count-Prince of Aragon use anachronisms and bombastic terminology. They speak of *els dos sobirans* (the two sovereigns), he of the 'Castilian State' and he of the 'Catalan-Aragonese State', and they call 'Catalan-Aragonese Confederation' what was always simply called Kingdom of Aragon. But leaving aside questions of nomenclature, we must not think that the history of Catalonia has been a huge mistake for the past eight centuries, but that the nationalists have written it mistakenly for the past forty years. It is they who misunderstand Catalonia, not Raymond Berenguer IV, nor the signers of the Compromise of Caspe. It is the separatists who fight against History by insisting on living alone, *Nosaltres sols*, when Catalonia never wished to live alone, but always united in a bilingual community with Aragon or with Castile.

THE LINGUISTIC QUESTION

In modern days, in the secessionist movements the greatest importance is given to diversity of language. While culture moves every day nearer to universal uniformity, greater value is given to the individual characteristics of many minor cultures based upon languages, whose historical development may be said to be incomplete, in comparison to the great cultural languages. The lively scientific and literary interest awakened in modern days in languages that were less studied before has acted as a support to the political interest taken in 'small nations'. But those whose interest is political do not appreciate how different is the part played by the great dominating languages to that played by those that have less substance, owing to the lack of so intense or original a culture or so continuous and unbroken a development. Flemish, Esthonian, Irish, Catalan come to represent political aspirations, and languages such as Basque which never were expressions of culture make desperate attempts to be so and achieve self-sufficiency. In short, there is a tendency to reduce the great cultural languages to the same historic level as the small ones, or even those which had no previous cultural existence.

In this connection we should note with regard to Spain that its superabundant Iberian individualism did not produce greater diversity of languages nor did this diversity operate in determining the historical disintegration which we have to record. If we take as a point of comparison a country so unified as France, we find far greater linguistic variety in each one of the regions, whether Breton, Basque, Gascon, Languedoc, Catalan, Franco-Provençal, French, Picard, as compared with Spanish Basque, Catalan, Gallego-Portuguese, Asturian, Leonese, Castilian and Upper-Aragonese. Abundant local variants comparable in number to those which are found all over the country in France and Italy can only be discovered in Asturias, Upper-Aragon, and in North Catalonia. So that Spain for all its individualistic traits is exceptional in being of great linguistic uniformity: it is in fact the Romanic country in which the diversity of dialects is least in relation to the extent of its territory.

There was one great unifying movement, namely the expansion of the Reconquest from north to south, which influenced both the linguistic elements and the general character of the people in a way that contradicts the theory of the disassociation caused by mountains and valleys. It all confirms the view that the causes of localism are not ethnological, psychological or linguistic differences, but rather the reverse, namely the uniformity of character, which is universally individualistic, in fact the Iberianism which Strabo describes as finding a difficulty in the very notion of solidarity.

Secondly, the differences of language had no influence on the process of subdivision which took place in the Middle Ages when this obeyed truly historical necessities. Language did not determine the formation of the kingdoms and counties in those days, and it was not taken into account. The Asturo-Leonese Kingdom was from the eighth century onwards a bilingual kingdom, for Galicia, which had no independent life, was always linked to it, and within this kingdom was established a series of administrative regions which were always bilingual likewise: namely, Asturias, El Bierzo, Sanabria. The three spoke Galician in their western and Leonese in their eastern divisions. The Kingdom of Navarre, from its beginning in the tenth century, used indifferently two spoken languages, Basque, and the Navarre dialect, which is akin to Castilian. For their written language only Latin and the Romance dialect were used, for Basque did not begin to be written at all until the sixteenth century. The capital, Pamplona, has spoken Castilian from mediaeval times. Even Castile itself was, from its origins, in the tenth century, a bilingual county or kingdom, for incorporated in its territory were both Alava and Biscay, already bilingual. Throughout practically all Alava, and the western half of Biscay up to the City of Bilbao itself and including it, the language spoken from time immemorial has been Castilian. The same may be said of the Kingdom of Aragon; from its beginning in the eleventh century it was bilingual owing to its county of Ribagorza, in whose eastern half Catalan is spoken, and the bilingualism of the kingdom asserted itself when in the twelfth century it was united to the great county of Barcelona. The county from that time onwards ceased to lead an isolated life and formed a single state with Aragon. As Rovira Virgili shows, the court or curia of the single monarch was a mixture of Aragonese and Catalan nobles, and the Cortes of the Kingdom was a mixed body frequently. The Kingdom of Valencia, finally, from its reconquest in the thirteenth century was bilingual and spoke both Catalan and Aragonese. Thus, during the many centuries when the centrifugal force of localism was on the increase, owing to the need for consolidating national life, we find bilingualism extending all over the country.

Consequently bilingualism, which has increased its effects owing to constant life in common, is to-day more intimate and more penetrating a force than in the Middle Ages. Castilian, as the language of authority, after having assimilated both the Leonese and Aragonese dialects, struck ever deeper roots as a cultural language in Catalan, Galician and Basque territory. Its greater activity as a literary medium of expression attracted not only the Basques, who always kept it as their written language, but also the others, for the literary use of Galician had practically ceased from the fifteenth century, and Catalan had noticeably diminished from the sixteenth century until in the nineteenth century the Romantic movement caused a rebirth of local cultures. Milá y Fontanals[1] in a lecture to the University of Barcelona reminded his audience of the enthusiasm for Calderón and

---

[1] Milá y Fontanals (1818–1884), Professor in the University of Barcelona, was the historian of Catalan as well as Castilian culture during the nineteenth century. One of the greatest authorities on mediaeval Castilian and Catalan literature.

the classical Spanish theatre shown in Catalonia, and he described how the plays were performed in cities and towns, and the sonorous, high-sounding verses were repeated with majestic emphasis by simple workmen. He concluded as follows: 'The Castilian language has been for us the language of a brother who has sat at our hearth and whose dreams we have mingled with our own.' And literary prestige makes itself felt not only in the exclusively learned productions of art, but also in the popular forms of wider appeal such as the traditional ballads so well known all through Catalonia and Galicia, either in Castilian versions sprinkled with Catalanisms or Galleguisms or else in Catalan and Galician versions full of Castilianisms. All this goes to prove how deep is the influence that cultural hegemony has over all social levels, over both learned and illiterate. The *Romancero*, which owes its beauty to its Castilian element as well as to its Catalan or Galician variants, comes to be a kind of everlasting plebiscite on behalf of the natural hispanic need for that intimate bilingualism which the autonomists reject as though it had been imposed by the arbitrary and intolerable tyranny of a central authority. This plebiscite of the *Romancero* is so alien to any centralism that the voting began from the early years of the fifteenth century at least, that is to say, long before the time when, through the union of Aragon and Castile, the latter could possibly have exercised any political pressure on Catalonia. Already about 1420 the traditional Castilian ballad, mixed with other Catalan poetical compositions, figured among the delightful literary curiosities which a Mallorcan student in Italy used to quote in order to evoke his distant Spanish fatherland. The nationalist, who is in revolt against these great facts of history, attempts to shake off the dull weight of history and subject his native tongue to a violent de-Castilianizing treatment. He would suppress the natural and universal linguistic phenomenon of borrowings and loans between two adjacent languages, mutual loans, though the less vigorous of the two is the greater debtor. Sometimes the nationalists, wishing to avoid a commonplace Castilian term of everyday usage, would select an uncommon expression which occasionally turned out to be itself a Castilianism in disguise. On other occasions they would invent a string of undigested neologisms. The whole plan was to pad out artificially the 'differentiating facts', do violence to nature, use the language as an instrument of political spite when it should be one of fraternal mutual comprehension, and poison the natural love that one has for the maternal tongue by inoculating the virus of envy. And the trouble is that the exaggerations of nationalism are often answered by the exaggeration of the defenders of centralization who even go as far as to forbid the reasonable and necessary use of the local language.

To sum up, the historical development of local languages and independent kingdoms in the past does not warrant us in believing that a difference of language is a natural cause of autonomy, nor that the intimate and popular bilingualism which has been practised by long tradition should be rejected as something imposed by the central power.

A TEMPORARY SUCCESS OF NATIONALISM

Nevertheless the ideas of the nationalists based on linguistics came to full fruition during the Second Republic. First of all approval was given to the Catalan Statute; then to the Basque Statute; and later the Galician Statute was to follow. There was a veritable craze for disintegration and a wish to build up a new structure for Spain, as if one were to break a jar against the wall in order to make a number of vessels with the potsherds. No anomaly of history was too far-fetched in order to separate what the centuries had always recognized as united. The Basques of the three Basque provinces, for example, even separated from their neighbours the Basques of Navarre, and wished to live alone though they had always lived in brotherly union with Castile. They invoked the claims of a language and a culture of their own. But, we may ask ourselves, what is Basque culture if not inseparably linked to Castilian for the glory of both? Basque did not begin to be written until the sixteenth century, and then only in exceedingly limited matters. If Saint Ignatius had not thought in Castilian more than in Basque he would never have been able to create his 'Spiritual Exercises', nor would he have been the universal Ignatius, but an obscure Iñigo, hidden away in his native mountains: if Elcano had not possessed a Castilian name and had not piloted a ship with a Castilian name at the service of ideals forged under Castilian hegemony, he would not have planned any maritime enterprise but that of fishing in the Bay of Biscay. In the same way we cannot even imagine the great Catalan or Galician heroes without setting them against the background of the kingdom of Aragon or Castile, any more than we can imagine the history of Castile or Aragon without those figures. Finally, during the Second as well as the First Republic, the tendency to subdivision appeared as the offshoot of the Republican ideology and, as in the days of Pí Margall, that tendency brought serious troubles to the Government, even to the point that severe measures had to be taken in Barcelona.

THE HISTORICAL THEORY OF UNITY AS AN ACCIDENTAL FORM

This contemporary federalism had like its predecessor a historical theory which is worth examining, as it is more fully developed than the former. It was most completely described in a speech delivered at Valencia during the Civil War in 1937 by the then rector of the University of Barcelona, the learned ethnologist, P. Bosch Gimpera. He examined the ethnological elements that inhabited the Peninsula, the fusion of even the most antagonistic elements through the effect of long periods of life in common, the events that had been shared together, and the part taken by the various peoples in the creation of determined spiritual values. He agreed that all this 'created a feeling of solidarity and a culture in common'; but as there exist underneath certain differences among the various elements that have fused together, while rejecting separatism, he defended the federalist policy of Pí Margall and Prat de la Riva which triumphed with the second republic. This difference of elements it is held, was not understood by historians, for up to to-day official and orthodox history, the Castilianizing history, is the history of the State, and the State is only an artificial *superstructure* imposed on the authentic Spain, that is to say, the Spain composed of primitive peoples. The superstructure which was imposed on those people by the Romans, the Goths, the Caliphate of Córdoba, the Austrian and Bourbon monarchies, was an artificial form which, though at times beneficial, in the long run was injurious, because it interrupted the flowering of the primitive stock, which is the essence of Spain. The Federalists wished to give life to this indigenous and genuine element of Spain, for they believed that unitarism limits itself to the superstructure.

This term *superstructure* (which, by the way, we find in Karl Marx) obliges us to consider its opposite: the indigenous basis which stubbornly reacts against the higher organization. This is bound to be an *infrastructure* which cannot represent what is eternally natural and authentic, but always something that is inferior to the superstructure, for though the latter at the beginning may have been artificial or imposed (it hardly ever was), yet it has been transformed by the work of centuries into an essential and authentic element. Let us take, for instance, in the case of Romanization, the first superstructure, its most artificial aspect, namely the expansion of Latin, which imposed itself and completely supplanted the various native languages. In the Latin implanted in the soil of the Peninsula and in the Romance language which succeeded it, all that survived as a poor *infra structure* were a few scanty relics of primitive languages. As a result, to-day it is only possible for us to think and live within the linguistic patterns given to us by the Roman elements, and the primitive Iberian tongue contributes but an occasional word or phrase mixed with the general Latin basis. The same is true of the principle of Hispanic unity. If Rome perfected and established it, thus perfected it incorporated itself in the Iberian spirit, once it had been confirmed by centuries of Gothic monarchy, the rule of the Caliphate and the years of unified monarchy ever since the fifteenth century. The mediaeval subdivisions and the brief modern revolts against the unity of the state belong to the *infrastructure* with its tendency to subdivide and split up. Though in the Middle Ages this saved the country from disaster, later on it became a destructive force even though it operated inconsistently and as a passing phase.

It is now supposed that all action directed against the superstructure was due to an outburst of primitive native forces in revolt against the artificial deformation which had been imposed upon them. Thus, for instance, the mediaeval kingdoms were the result of pre-Roman nuclei which could not be dominated and which rose up in revolt. But the true story is that the structure of pre-Roman Spain is all but unknown to us, and even where we do possess some knowledge of it, we have to leave it aside and turn our main attention to the Roman or Visigothic period, that is to say to the superstructure. When attempts are made to explain why Valencia became Castilianized more rapidly than Catalonia, the reason given is that a Celtic element, akin to that of Castile, stretched from Celtiberia to Segorbe, a region where to-day Aragonese and not Valencian is spoken. But this identification of Segorbe with the *Segobriga caput Celtiberiae* of Pliny cannot be accepted, among other reasons because it is based only upon a resemblance of names, and this resemblance disappears when we learn that in the Middle Ages the form was Soborbe, not Segorbe. Segobriga, the capital of Celtiberia, must be placed in Cuenca, on the hill known as Cabeza del Griego. The proximate cause of the rapid Castilianization of Valencia was that it was reconquered, half by the Aragonese, half by the Catalans, and the remote cause must be sought not in ethnography, of which we know hardly anything, but in the administrative systems current in Roman, Visigothic and Moslem times when Valencia was a suffragan diocese of Toledo. It was for this reason that the Archbishop of Toledo claimed jurisdiction over the Valencian churches reconquered by James I. The Castilian spirit of Valencia thus goes back to the superstructure, not to the contact the Celts had with the primitive Edetani. The same is true for the mediaeval kingdoms. We cannot explain them as the result of the rising of indigenous nuclei which are either unknown to us, or have no connection with these kingdoms. On the other hand we find that they do coincide in some points with certain details of the Roman-Gothic superstructure which is known to us, as for instance, the extension of Navarre under Sancho el Mayor as far as the Oca mountains which were the boundary of the ancient Tarraconensis province. It is easy to explain why historians are always interested in the superstructure seeing that it is this that gives to the people its most complete and elaborate system of life. It is the work of representative men produced by the people itself or the assimilation by them of influences from outside. We do not deny that the action of what we call the *infrastructure* may also be the object of history, but this *infrastructure* must not be taken as the essential form of the Spanish people hampered in its growth by the superstructure. If the superstructure were only a deformation, and if it had been supported under protest not only as far back as the time of Raymond Berenguer IV but as far back as Rome itself, that is to say 2,000 years ago, we should have to conclude that the Spanish people had shown an inconceivable passivity which amounted to non-existence. But let us be clear on this point: the form of life of the Spaniards throughout these 2,000 years has not been a perpetual mistake, nor was the superstructure artificial; it was in fact the normal structure, the most natural one that the Spanish people could select in the particular historical circumstances in which it was involved.

LOCALISM AS AN ACCIDENTAL DISEASE

The mediaeval kingdoms served their purpose and endured because they grew up gradually in opposition to adverse forces from without which were attempting to disrupt violently the ancient, well-consolidated unity. They came into being and maintained themselves as a defence against threatening catastrophe. On the contrary the federalism, cantonalism, and nationalism of modern days have come to destroy the unity of many centuries and have not succeeded in establishing themselves. Far from representing authentic Spain they belong only to an abnormal and transitory moment, a period of weakness that cannot be prolonged without grave danger to the country. They appear as a disease which attacks a nation, when its strength is low, for all disease consists in the struggle for autonomy of some organ which refuses to co-operate with the unified functioning of the body. Localism has always existed side by side with unitarism, but in moments of pathological weakness both one and the other become exacerbated. Differences of temperament, language, interests between the component parts exist in every nation, but in Spain these are felt with peculiar acuteness owing to the difficulty of understanding the long-term advantages of association. On the other hand, in the unified state there often is a failure to appreciate the problems of the region; there is, in fact, a lack of that strong and just spirit of co-ordination whereby each part of the nation feels itself assisted in a way which it is forced to recognize as equitable. Sometimes what happens is that extravagant concessions are made to the autonomous regions, and they are given protection which injures the other regions.

On other occasions there is a severe repression of legitimate aspirations and attempts are made to suppress violently the symptoms of the disease without trying to cure it at its roots by wise and steadfast government.

Chapter V

The Two Spains

It is not only the struggle of the localist spirit against the spirit of unity that weakens national cohesion. We must also bear in mind the unusual vehemence in which differences of political ideology separate Spaniards from one another, thus breaking down the moral unity of the mass of the people. This needs two preliminary explanations.

ISOLATION AND COMMUNICATIONS

The element of austerity in the Spaniard's character, with its lack of interest in novelties, leads him to pay little heed to the spiritual currents that flourish in the more advanced countries. This is the reason why Spaniards so fiercely oppose one another, some advocating isolation from the outside world, others, on the contrary, considering it necessary to establish active intellectual communications with those foreign peoples who lead in culture. The personification of this struggle is Padre Feijóo, who was unwearying in his fight against isolation.

In these alternations between activity and passivity, the tendency to retire into seclusion predominates. The clearest proof of how far the spirit of seclusion prevails may be found in the peculiar lack of interest of the Spaniard in travel. Saavedra Fajardo laments bitterly that there is no taste for 'wandering, the mistress of Prudence'. He adds that northern nations are to be praised for their curiosity, 'which leads them to reconnoitre the world and learn languages, arts and sciences. Spaniards, who with greater ease than the rest could become acquainted with the world, seeing that their rule extends on all sides, are those who remain in closest seclusion in their countries, unless when the call of arms drives them abroad.'

This lack of the spirit of travel becomes a serious limitation. The Venetian ambassador Paolo Tiepolo,[1] when describing the Court of Philip II in 1562, makes a distinction between the Spaniards who have never left their country and those who have travelled in foreign lands. The first, he says, 'do not try to understand anything beyond what they see, and what they have learnt from their nurses, and thus they utter the strangest and most unreasonable statements imaginable: the others, on the contrary, are prudent, wise, tolerant, and always attend to what is honourable no less than what is useful'. This substantial difference, noted by Tiepolo, is one which has always existed. Even though one need not be as bitter as the Venetian in describing the stay-at-homes, yet we always note a radical difference between the Spaniard, whether he be scientist, priest or industrialist or whatever else, who has travelled, and the man who is satisfied to live in isolation. Unfortunately to-day there is the same exaggerated unwillingness to move about noted by Saavedra Fajardo; even more so, for to-day that extensive monarchy no longer exists nor those foreign wars. Amongst the many who are aware of this disease let us take the case of the Countess Pardo Bazán. Realizing that she was an out-and-out Spaniard she imposed upon herself the following precept: just as the Church orders us to confess our sins once a year, so culture ought to order every Spaniard to go outside his country once a year, and more than once, if he notes in himself any symptoms of mental stagnation. But if a wise law were to lay down that those who did not carry out more or less the cultural precept of the Countess Pardo Bazán should not be allowed to hold administrative posts, Spain would remain without rulers. For all that, it is clear that the habit of travel is not always a sure test; the only essential point is to feel the necessity of getting into intimate spiritual intimacy with the foreigner. There are some who feel this keenly and yet have never left their country, as was the case of Padre Feijóo, and there are others who travel as their trunk does. But in the end, with or without travel, the fact is that isolation prevails in Spain and seeks to justify itself on the principle that the Spaniard has

[1] The illustrious Venetian family of Tiepolo rendered great services in diplomacy. One of the family, Paolo Tiepolo, who was killed in 1585, was Ambassador in Spain, 1560, and also in France and Rome. The Account of his Embassy in Spain is dated 1562.

very little to learn from foreign peoples and that it is most
essential to preserve unimpaired all the traditional forms of life
and thought and keep them free from any contact with foreign
influences which would only weaken them and imperil their
existence. All Feijóo's diatribes against those two prejudices
have as much meaning to-day as they had in his time.

EXCLUSIVENESS AND TOLERANCE

That same austerity which dominates the Spanish character
may be the cause of the poverty of its impressions and reactions.
There is an absorbing interest in what is considered the principal
thing in life, and indifference towards what is considered of
secondary importance, that is to say, complete absorption in one
object, and disregard of anything else. This is a great quality in
the case of enthusiastic action, but a great failing, even perilously
near negligence, when dealing with the many connecting causes
that make up the complexities of life. In this way the restriction
of interest goes to the opposite extreme of exaggeration. Pliny,
who had been an imperial procurator in the Peninsula, and was
well acquainted with the Spaniards, attributes to them two
principal qualities: physical endurance and vehemence of spirit,
vehementia cordis. Donoso Cortés[1] said, most aptly, that 'the
historical characteristic of the Spaniard is to exaggerate in
everything.'

Spaniards are always prone to exaggerate. Either they are in
the depths of depression and consider themselves inferior to the
rest of the world, or else they reach the extremes of national pride
and believe that they are the new Chosen People. Their climax
of power in history was magnificent and exhausting, an exclusive
consecration to a high ideal upheld in opposition to the most
powerful adversaries with a complete disregard of their own
wants and necessities.

The same exclusive trait and the same disregard for their most
urgent needs occur in their internal disputes. Every Spaniard is
prone to consider his own opinion as the only one possible. Those

---

[1] Juan Donoso Cortés, 1809–1853, Marquis of Valdegamas, was at first a liberal,
but later evolved towards rigid Catholicism which he explained in his book
Ensayo sobre el catolicismo, el liberalismo y el socialismo, 1851.

who differ from him he merely despises, if the matter is of secondary importance, and he betrays not the slightest curiosity to know about them; if the differences are capital he immediately condemns them as intolerable, without taking into account the good points which must always exist in any diversity of opinion, no matter how wide of the mark it may be. He is unable to conceive the fruitful co-existence of discrepant principles, worthy of respect as containing some possibility of being right. As a result, in Spain difference of opinion degenerates into a contest of irreconcilable animosity.

Larra, during a critical period of the nineteenth century, imagined the mortal struggle as taking place between the two halves of Spain, an idea which Fidelino de Figueiredo expanded in a fine book of ample historical vision, '*As duas Espanhas*'. In that book he described the struggle which began in the eighteenth century between the two tendencies, namely whether the direction given to national life by Philip II should be re-established or abolished. This tragic dualism in Spain is so true that we must consider it extending back beyond these two centuries, in fact, all through Spanish history, for it is a necessary result of the inborn tendency to extremes that we have described. The struggle between opposite tendencies, especially between tradition and innovation, is the normal state in all peoples; but in Spain this struggle occurs regularly in a most bitter form whereas it only takes place at critical moments in other countries. Here, in Spain, frequently no agreement can be arrived at by both tendencies, especially with regard to the most urgent and vital problems which arise, because the Iberian Peninsula is either exposed to the influences that pour in from the two continents which she links together, or else she retires into the isolation that is due to her remote geographical position.

This struggle between different tendencies should be carefully noted as it appears in the different historical epochs, for it has consumed a great part of the historical energy of the Spanish people, but to the truce in the struggle, when the two opposite forces managed to unite in harmony, we owe the most fruitful moments of national life.

BETWEEN AFRICA AND EUROPE

One of the taunts that has been repeated most often by foreign countries is that which compares Spain to Africa. It was already referred to by Feijóo and formulated later by Alexander Dumas: 'Africa begins at the Pyrenees.' Unamuno, influenced by Martin Hume's unfortunate 'History of the Spanish People', converted this taunt into a formulation of a programme, by proposing the preferential cultivation of those qualities which distinguish the Spanish people from its neighbours in Europe. This he did because he considered that the affirmation of the Africanism of Spain was the first step in a process of evaluation which would one day lead to the influence of Spain on the other modern peoples. We, on our side, answer that although we are unable to recognize the African elements that Hume and Unamuno discover in this or that Spanish quality, nevertheless the Africanization of Spain at different periods was a historical process which repeated itself more often than is believed, only that it does not imply a difference or an inferiority to western culture, but rather the reverse.

On the occasion of the Punic wars we learn for the first time how the two Spains faced each other, one of them the ally of Hannibal and the other of the Scipios. Early in the struggle Spain decides its European destiny from the moment when the Saguntines sacrifice themselves to preserve their Roman alliance—so extremely heroic an act that it was not even fully understood by the Romans themselves (*'fidem socialem usque ad perniciem suam coluerunt'*, says Livy in a tone of wondering admiration). And this Punic Africa, Africa Minor, after being the seat of Carthaginian culture and the dread rival of Latin culture, became one of the most prosperous provinces of the Roman Empire. When political and intellectual power had passed from the Italians to the inhabitants of the provinces, after the Hispanic century which stretches from Mela and Seneca to Trajan and Hadrian, there came the period from the second to the fourth century when Africa took the lead with Apuleius, Septimius Severus, Tertullian, Saint Cyprian, Arnobius, Saint Augustine, and Martianus Capella. This period was followed by the hegemony of Gaul, between the fourth and the sixth centuries.

This Africa, so noble a portion of Western Latin civilization, lived on a par with Spain, not in opposition to, but in deep community with all the culture of Christian Europe. Africanism then meant the same in Spain as Europeanism did later, that is to say the tendency to shake off cultural isolation. To this Africa the Galician Paulus Orosius travelled in order to receive inspiration from the great father of the Church, Saint Augustine, and in the following centuries, even when intellectual supremacy passed back to Spain, during the period of Saint Isidore, the African Church continued in close relations with the Visigothic. This inclination towards Christian Africa is clearly visible in the historical treatise of Saint Isidore, '*De Viris Illustribus*', where, among the religious men of recent memory there commemorated, he sets next the fourteen from Spain, eleven from Africa, another eleven from Italy, while he mentions only four names from Gaul. The Spain of Saint Isidore, which was in such close relationship with Africa, casts a brilliant beam, the last before the beacon of antiquity was extinguished over the dark ages. It was the Iberian Peninsula, the link between the two continents, that under the influence of the Hispano-Roman Saint Isidore produced the last flowering of Latin-Mediterranean culture which was to be followed by the long period of collapse until Latin-German culture began to bloom in the centre of Europe.

In the political history of that Visigothic age one can also perceive an opposition between the Spain that unites itself to Byzantine Africa and the other which leans upon the Frankish Kingdom, and doubtless to this dualism was due the ferocious partisan spirit which destroyed the Gothic monarchy in its last seventy years. In vain the clergy in its Toledan councils tried to exercise a moderating influence over the extremes that were at war with one another, by urging the kings to use pity and indulgence rather than vengeance and cruelty with their opponents, so that they might be able to rely on the hearts of their subjects against external enemies. In vain were those warnings included in full in the '*Lex Visigothorum*' as an urgent necessity in the government of the kingdom; the antagonism between the two halves raged implacably, and the confiscations and murders reached such a pitch of violence that the Frankish historian Fredegarius gave it the name of 'Gothic disease', thus signifying the grafting of German roughness on to Hispanic exaggeration. The irreconcilable duel reaches its tragic end with the handing over of the kingdom to external enemies, when the family of Vitiza asked for help from Africa.

By that time the conquest of Africa by the Arabs had gravely disturbed the balance of life in all the Western Mediterranean, especially in Spain. Africa with its magnificent Latin civilization and its profound Christian spirit, so admired by Saint Isidore, had become Islamic Africa, torn away from the western world to be united henceforth to the Asiatic East. The party of Vitiza, helped by the Africans, were the victors, and drove the partisans of King Roderick to seek narrow refuge in the mountains of Asturias. The counts and bishops of Vitiza who are personified in the famous Julian and Opas reached such a pitch of arrogant intolerance that, setting their party before everything, they did not hesitate to enslave their religion and their country by handing them over to the Moslem auxiliaries. Half of Spain annihilated the other half, but Spain in its entirety fell into Mozarabic serfdom beneath the African yoke.

When little by little the defeated party rose again in Asturias, the only survivor of free Spain, we must not think of a partisan movement of opposition, but of a struggle between two states that occupy separate territories and have separate and distinct governments. Southern Spain, *El Andalús*, although it developed an Islamism that was, to a great degree, Hispanized in customs, art and ideology, remained in isolation from Europe and united to the Afro-Asiatic cultural world. Northern Spain, though steadfast in its Christian spirit, nevertheless was subjected to a great degree to the influences from the south, at a time when Arabic culture was far superior to Latin, and it then accomplished its high historical mission of being the link between the two worlds of the east and the west.

EUROPEANISM AND MEDIAEVAL 'CASTICISMO'

Later, when the cultural superiority of the Arab world over the Latin world ceased, once the inrush from the south had spent itself, there was no question of a struggle between the influences from Africa and those from Europe. Nevertheless, in the north the struggle between two tendencies and two Spains began under different conditions. Only one of the two continents to which the Iberian peninsula serves as a link is now important, but the influences from European life reach her late because of her remote position, a distant shore to which only the strongest waves could reach, leaving behind many others to break on nearer shores. And frequently adverse historical circumstances produced long periods of life apart from, and in disagreement with, the rest of the West. And every time that the isolation ceases or diminishes the results of this separation are felt; the struggle breaks out between those wishing to correct the effects of isolation, by adapting the life of the Peninsula to that of the rest of Europe, and those of the opposite tendency who wish to maintain intact the ancestral heritage of culture.

The longest period of isolation which Spain suffered with regard to Europe was that caused by the hegemony of Moslem Córdoba, from the eighth to the tenth century inclusive. Already at the beginning of that hegemony, Northern Spain, the offspring of Mediterranean culture, that is to say, of Graeco-Latin antiquity, felt itself cut off from the new nordic culture of Latin-German origin which had begun in the Europe of the Carolingian dynasty. The relations between Alfonso the Chaste and Charlemagne imply the existence of a primitive party of *afrancesados*, as they used to say in the eighteenth century, or *europeizantes*, as they said in the nineteenth, and from their opposition to the rest of their countrymen sprang the legend of Bernardo del Carpio. Precise information on those primitive parties can only be found in the eleventh century, referring to the ecclesiastical reforms and the substitution of the Roman rite for that of Saint Isidore.

This is the most typical example of the cultural isolation produced by Spain's remote geographical position. She had given great splendour to a national Church which was a glorious example owing to its ancient councils, its discipline, its liturgy, its hymns and its sacred music, but as a result of its traditional isolation it was unable in its succeeding evolution to influence the liturgical development of the universal Church, as might have been expected, owing to its own high qualities, nor did it manage to take its share in the general evolution. For this reason, after four centuries had passed, it found itself at loggerheads with Rome when Gregory VII, with the help of the monks from Cluny, proposed to unify the rite. The remedy for such prolonged isolation was bound to be difficult and hard, a noble and much-loved portion of tradition had to be uprooted, and it was necessary to receive a host of foreign clerics, who would implant the new patterns of ecclesiastical life intended to replace the national ones. At this time Sancho el Mayor of Navarre and his two grandsons, Sancho Ramírez in Aragon and Alfonso VI in Castile, as well as the Cid in Valencia, became 'Europeanizers' in the sense that they led the party which favoured the introduction of the reforms imposed by Rome and the occupation of the principal ecclesiastical posts by the monks of Cluny. We know that there was a traditionalist party, very hostile to these reforms, and its stubborn opposition in defence of the Toledan rite showed itself in 'judgements of God', trials by combat and court intrigues. The bitter struggle between traditionalist and innovating Spain in this liturgical question is known to us because it was of great interest to the clerical historians of those days. But with the exception of this episode which concerns the religious sphere, we know nothing of similar episodes which must have occurred then in other spheres of life.

Because of its connection with the liturgy, we have one piece of evidence which enables us to say that, broadly speaking, the Europeanizing party in its triumph behaved in no violent or authoritarian way towards the opposite party, but with considerable moderation. I refer to the substitution of French for Visigothic script. By virtue of this change all the books of the Hispanic past became illegible, and thus the cultural continuity of the country was cut off and a new era began in which all Spanish books would have to be rewritten in the new script and the majority of them would be substituted by others copied from those in other countries. But this change was, generally speaking, carried out very gradually and spontaneously. Alfonso VI and the Cid continued to use in their chancelleries the Visigothic lettering; only in prayer books was there an ordinance imposing French lettering, but in all other documents the change was made in special instances and took thirty years to accomplish, a fact which indicates a gradual acceptance on the part of the traditionalist party. This signifies that there was a spirit of accommodation, which, when applied to all orders of life, was the cause of the great prosperity of this period. The sorrowful determination to sacrifice the past, a feeling which would seem inconceivable in modern days to the traditionalists in Spain, but was welcomed in those days by the noblest figures of the early Spanish Middle Ages, was taken in order that Spain might make up for its former long period of isolation and incorporate itself into the life of Europe, but it was carried out after securing a happy agreement between two antagonistic parties. Spain renounced a great part, indeed a glorious part, of its past, and yet kept its own spirit which enabled it to create its greatest poetical hero in the person of one of those innovators. The '*Poema del Cid*' welcomed the all-powerful French influence and gave it a typically Spanish poetic form, and at the same time, with a noble spirit that was ethical as well as artistic, renewed the ideal of epic poetry both Spanish and French. Spain lived in this period of renunciation in its last heroic age, the most original of them all and the most magnificent.

In the following two centuries we can readily note the continued influence of Spain as an innovator, when numerous Frankish colonies were established in the principal cities of the Peninsula; when Alfonso VII appeared as a modernizing king imposing feudal principles on the ancient empire of León, and generously welcoming to his court the Provençal troubadours; when at the same time Archbishop Raymond of Toledo encouraged the founding of schools where Arab, Jewish and Christian scholars collaborated in a series of works, which, when communicated to the learned centres in Europe, opened a new era in mediaeval science. Soon afterwards the poets of León, Rioja and Aragon imported from France a perfect syllabic form of verse,[1] boasting that it was superior to the primitive Spanish metre. This reform was similar to the one so much resisted by Cristóbal de Castillejo, when it was a question of Italian influence.

Immediately afterwards came Alfonso X who gathered into

[1] The metrical reform introduced from France by Gonzalo de Berceo about 1230 was the stanza of alexandrines or lines of twelve syllables. The reform attacked by Castillejo (1490–1550) was the hendecasyllabic Italian line of verse introduced by Garcilaso (1503–1536) about 1525.

his court the learned of the three religions, for he was as eager to sift the wisdom of the East as of the West and paid as much attention to the new Roman Law as he did to the old laws and customs of Spain. He was the first European king interested in secularizing culture, which he did by expressing his vast encyclopaedic knowledge in a vulgar Romance tongue. An echo of the violent opposition that was aroused by his audacious novelties still reaches us to-day when we read of how he was reputed to be an impious blasphemer. But all the opposition against reform was unable to prevent his success, and his historical and legal works were translated by scholars all over Spain into Catalan and into Portuguese. His oriental works were translated into French and had an influence on Dante. The Astronomical Tables were studied in Europe for various centuries and were read and annotated by Copernicus himself. During all this great movement of the twelfth and thirteenth centuries, now that the forces working for innovation and those working for tradition were happily reconciled, Spain underwent a deep transformation and reached one of her historical peak points. She assimilated the abundant influences of the East as well as those from Europe, and she accomplished in the most brilliant way her true destiny, which was to serve as a link between the two heterogeneous worlds of Christianity and Islam. At the same time that an impulse was given to traditional institutions whether social or political, she carried on the century-old war to recover the soil of the fatherland. In that war the greatest conqueror of all was one who was both king and saint, Ferdinand III, and whose epitaph, written in different languages, proclaims him to be a king who was tolerant to infidel cults in mosque and synagogue.

UNIFICATION: THE DUAL CHARACTER OF THIS EPOCH

As a contrast to the magnificent development during the epoch of Alfonso VII and Alfonso X we must recall another powerful influx of new ideas and customs, strangely contemptuous of the traditional foundations of public life. The general decadence caused by the break up of the Middle Ages reduced Spain to a very low level of depression, and this was increased by the degenerate character of Henry IV. The throne itself set the foolish example of belittling and insulting all national feelings. Moorish customs were openly adopted; the war of reconquest was wilfully impeded; scorn of the laws was actively encouraged and corruption became the order of the day among all the officers of government and justice. Religion was openly jeered at, and people boasted of their bestial materialism, while at court the immoral practices became a public scandal.

The traditionalist party at first showed their opposition by proclaiming the anti-king Alfonso; afterwards they chose Isabel, Princess of Asturias. And the great success of the movement personified by Isabel consisted in not limiting the reaction to a mere party movement, but in a prudent uniting of all the forces at their disposal. The characteristic quality of the Catholic monarchs was their earnest determination to select the right man for the right place, which prompted them both to attract to their side even their enemies, converting them into collaborators, and to co-ordinate and harmonize the two antagonistic tendencies. Once this double task had been carried out, traditional Spain succeeded in restoring all her values, which before this had been perversely and wantonly tramped underfoot. With exemplary zeal law and morality were made the rule for the people, and social order was reimposed after an implacable internal war had been waged against the powerful elements of disorder and anarchy. It was then decided to complete once and for all the conquest of Granada, and undertake the reforms which would raise the dignity of the religious institutions. But through all this restoration of tradition the spirit of reforming Spain was present, introducing elements of perfection which had been unknown before. A notable example was the new plan adopted for organizing and directing the war against Granada. Another was the admission of the middle class into the high administrative posts. Above all we should mention the firm anti-isolationist policy which attracted to Spain all the modern currents of the European Renaissance. The former uncouth barbarism was now combated by Spanish humanists educated abroad, and by learned Italians, French, Greeks and Jews invited to court, to the noble houses and to the Universities of Alcalá and Salamanca. The young nobles, who formerly led a life of slothful ease, were now obliged by the Queen to attend the classes given by these foreign scholars. And so, all through these acts of the monarchs we notice a desire for culture and education, and this culminates in the decree of 1480 which enacted that works of the intellect should be imported into the country free of customs dues, tithes and all other taxes, for it was seen that the merchants 'every day brought in good books in great quantities and this redounds to the profit of all and ennobles our kingdoms'. This enthusiastic and continuous attempt to harmonize and make full use of both tendencies is the true cause of the immediate prosperity that ensued.

In addition to all this work of co-ordinating the elements which had operated in the past, we should lay special stress upon a new and prevailing thought of the Catholic monarchs, which, although it, too, was rooted in the Middle Ages, yet was more decidedly directed towards modern times. The tendencies towards absolute kingly power and the national personality of the State, both of them aspirations which the Renaissance inculcated into princes, became more prominent in the Catholic monarchs, and with truly Spanish originality they fused these ideas with the mediaeval universalist idea which the national states with their local ideas of autonomy were trying their best to combat. The Spanish state would henceforth be based upon the unity of the Catholic faith and its ever-increasing propagation. And this design, owing to the grandeur of its scope, prevails over all others if it meets opposition. Thus the broad, tolerant spirit of the Middle Ages, practised by the great kings, who were both warriors and saints, ends now with the expulsion of the Jews and the violent baptism of the Moors of Granada *en masse*, to which must be added the new system of the Inquisition which had been set up. This implantation of religious intolerance at the end of the fifteenth century is the great change which divides the history of the characteristically Spanish cult of extremes into two completely distinct epochs. At the beginning, under the Catholic monarchs, intolerance was necessary to a certain extent in order to unify the nation in its European spirit by the suppression of foreign religions. Nevertheless, it is also worth noting that the cautious attitude towards Europe, with regard to printed books, makes its first appearance in 1502, in contrast with the confident optimism of twenty years before. It was now necessary to get a previous government licence to sell or print books, under penalty of a heavy fine and disqualification. This restriction by censorship was at the start a mild one, but as time went on it was to grow more severe and became the favourite method to be followed by those who aimed at intellectual isolationism.

THE INCREASE UNDER CHARLES V

In spite of these restrictions, during the period of Charles V isolationism was suppressed as never before. The price paid for this suppression was indeed heavier than in the period of Alfonso VI to which we referred before. The two aspects of abnormal intensity which we mentioned then as characteristic of such great changes, namely the influx of foreign counsellors and the violent attacks made on important traditional principles, were now to be witnessed in full force. First of all we have the inrush of Flemish followers in the suite of the grandson of the Catholic monarchs when he entered Spain, then we have the overthrow of vital political institutions after the defeat of the Comuneros at Villalar[1] and the substitution of new forms of government. But in the midst of the fierce struggle, young Charles heard from his own followers the crudest and most humiliating truths, which induced him to substitute for the violence shown at the beginning a respect and love for Spain. Thus it was the War of the Communes which caused the Hispanization of the Emperor, and the consequent enthusiastic association of Spain with the vast imperial plans. As a result there came about an active and fruitful interchange between Spaniards and foreigners in the government, in the army, in the court, and in all orders of life.

Charles V, a staunch Catholic as well as tolerant by nature, was the best fitted to be the leader of this the greatest and most spontaneous opening of the Spanish mind to all the problems that were agitating the world, and the result was that the spirit of Spain extended its influence over all fields of action in Europe and in America, in its aspiration towards *One Monarch, one Empire, and one Sword*. At that time the history of Spain became

[1] Villalar was the place where, on 23 April 1521, the Comuneros were defeated. They had tried to impose upon Charles V the authority of the Castilian Cortes. The war of the *Communidades* lasted one and a half years.

the history of the universe in the old world as well as in that which had been recently discovered.

When he perceived that all his plans for saving the spiritual unity of Europe had failed, Charles retired to Yuste, but although isolationism then began, Spain still continued to be the centre of universal history during the greater part of the reign of Philip II.

EXCLUSIVENESS PREDOMINATES

Philip II on assuming with determination the decision to maintain the Catholic unity of Europe counted upon the loyal adhesion of a traditionalist majority who saw their ancient convictions linked with the extraordinary political development of the nation which now had reached the summit of its power. This great triumph caused the spiritual unity of the Spaniards to increase its strength daily, and to maintain it they needed, at all costs, to preserve it from dangerous ideas that were current in other countries, those, in fact, against which they were fighting. But the precautions they took ended by being altogether out of all proportion. In the early years of his reign, in 1558, Philip II prohibited, under penalty of death and confiscation, the importation and publication of books without a licence from the State Council, lest those books might contain heresies, new-fangled notions against the faith, or 'vain matters' that might give evil example. Let us note how the penalty had increased, for in 1502 it only consisted in a fine and disqualification. In the following year, 1559, Philip II also prohibited Spaniards from studying abroad except at Rome, Naples or Coimbra, or in the Spanish college at Bologna. He gave two reasons for these restrictions: first because Spanish universities 'are daily diminishing and in bankruptcy'; that is to say, he took the absence of the students as a cause, whereas it was only an effect, of the bad state in which the Spanish universities found themselves. The second reason was that the intercourse with foreigners involved the students in extravagance, dangers and distractions. And so, as he did not find in the world any universities free from dangers except those at home or practically at home, he closed the doors and windows of the decayed Spanish schools so that the inmates might breathe nothing but their own confined air.

Nevertheless, though this was the period during which Spain reached one of its moments of greatest unanimity, yet the conformity was to a large extent only apparent, and was possible owing to the severe repression carried out by the enemies of progressive thought who were ready to persecute the slightest trace of non-conformity, even the new ideas, not in any way heretical, of a Fray Luis de León or a Brocense, [1] at whose trials the crowd of domineering reactionaries had actually to be restrained by the tribunal of the Inquisition itself. And in spite of the unanimity which had been achieved we can observe some deep divergencies of opinion, even with regard to the central idea of Counter-Reformation policy, namely the religious repression in Flanders, though the dissenting element was only able to operate within very reduced limits.

The theologians, who were first consulted in 1565, gave it as their opinion that, taking into account the dangers that would ensue for the Church from the rebellion and imminent war, the King might, without any danger to his royal conscience, allow the cities of Flanders to have the freedom of worship they asked for. But Philip II, declaring himself opposed to this opinion, swore that he would never allow the religious unity to be broken, for he did not wish to be lord over heretics who did such offence against God. In this the King, more zealous than the theologians, was interpreting faithfully the opinion of the great majority of his subjects. The man charged with the carrying out of his inflexible zeal was the Duke of Alba, who, swayed by his self-denying loyalty to the crown, insisted upon bearing the responsibility for all the odium which his severity would arouse. By displaying his accustomed harshness he carried out to the entire satisfaction of his master the repressive policy which the King was determined to carry to the bitter end. The Duke summed up the reasons for this policy in a biting phrase: 'It is far better to preserve by war for God and the King a kingdom that is impoverished and even ruined than, without the war, preserve it entire for the benefit of the devil and the heretics, his disciples.'

Pirenne believes that if the Duke of Alba had been twenty

---

[1] Francisco Sánchez (El Brocense), reviver of Spanish humanism, was professor of Greek and Latin at the University of Salamanca during the last quarter of the sixteenth century. He and Fray Luis de León were accused to the Inquisition by the rigid elements dominating the University of Salamanca at that time.

years younger he would not have thought thus; for his thoughts were those of the ancient Spaniards who had been trained in the holy war against the Moors. This is not the case. This was no mere archaic conception, but the usual Hispanic exaggeration backed up in this case by the unbounded passions which were stirred up in Europe by the religious question among both Catholics and Protestants. Philip II was twenty years younger in accordance with Pirenne's dictum, but he was as rigid in his views as Alba or more so. Gregory IX considered the Massacre of Saint Bartholomew as a fortunate day for Catholicism. We, therefore, must not blame in any way the severity of the first decision that was taken. The error of Philip II was in not seeing that, when it came to repressing ideas, if he did not succeed with the employment of violence once and for all at the outset, he would never do so, but would make the situation worse by keeping up so constant a policy of executions that it became endemic, for blood that has been spilt serves but the one purpose of making proselytes for its cause. And to the error of the King we must add the error of the majority of the Spanish people.

This majority paid no attention to a considerable minority which foresaw the future, namely that the Low Countries, driven into poverty and ruin, would be shared out between God and the heretics, under worse conditions with war than would have been the case without war. Many Spaniards, some of them very distinguished men, saw this coming. Arias Montano, from 1568 on, and above all in 1573, disapproved of the harsh repression carried out by Alba, especially in the case of the punishments inflicted at Naarden and Zutphen. That cruel war, he said, was just a squandering of many millions and 'the loss of countless souls and lives of Spaniards as well as of the enemy'. It was an urgent necessity that the Council of Troubles[1] should not serve merely for the purpose of chastising the rebellious, but should also raise the moral tone of the corrupt Spanish administration and enable His Majesty to recapture the affection of his vassals. Likewise the Secretary Esteban Prats asserted in 1572 that the sackings carried out by the soldiery, added to their extortions, violence, raping and vile deeds, 'had been the chief cause (not heresy as some tried

---

[1] *El Consejo de los Tumultos* was the French *Conseil des Troubles*. It was distinguished by its rigour in putting down disturbances.

to prove) for driving the Flemish people into despair'. Similarly, Don Francisco de Alava, the Prince of Eboli, the royal chronicler Furío Ceriol, and many others, condemned the war which the Duke of Alba was waging as a tragic error, and they maintained that more thought should be given to Spanish maladministration than to heresy.

The opposition against the war extended all over Castile, because this was the kingdom that paid the heaviest amount of tribute, and even though it was dangerous to oppose it because of the King's decision to carry on, there were protests on all sides. At the end of the reign, when the money had still to be found for war and the finances of the country were exhausted, it was decided, about January 1595, to impose a new tribute on flour. Then there was published an anonymous pamphlet, attributed with certainty to the jurist Gonzalo de Valcárcel, which courageously stated the point of view of the minority: if God has abandoned England and Flanders for their sins, we shall gain nothing by killing heretics, while without any war at all God preserved Bavaria from heresy. The many religious wars that Spain has fought since the days of Charles V against Germany, France, England, and Flanders show that the patient is not to be cured with that medicine; in fact it is a proof that the cure is a failure: 'What has our paying the flour tax here to do with making them give up their heresies over there? Can it be that France, Flanders, and England will be more virtuous in proportion as Spain is poorer? A remedy for the sins of Nineveh[1] was not found by increasing the tribute in Palestine so as to pay for the expedition to conquer them, but rather in sending there some one who would convert them.' And the anonymous protest adds: 'It is said that Castile is long-suffering and will bear all the burden, but it has no longer the strength: the towns are becoming depopulated, the estates are lying fallow, the farmers flee to the mountains as they cannot pay the tributes.' This dark picture and these arguments show how damaged materially and how reasonable intellectually was this dissenting portion of Spain's population. They obtained the trifling satisfaction of foiling the flour tax, not by their arguments, for these met with no response, but owing to the widespread exhaustion of the country.

[1] An allusion to the Old Testament, Book of Jonah.

We have regarded it as quite natural that in the beginning a severe repressive system should have been used against the dissenters, for this was the prevailing one everywhere in the baroque period; but, later on, even the extreme limit of poverty which Spain reached was not enough to impose the opinion of the minority in the face of the war party which remained impregnable and immutable in its high resolve. The thought of making Spain the champion of the unity of the faith was certainly one of noble abnegation, and it enabled Spain to preserve for modern Europe a precious reserve of Catholic spirit, of moral values, all in fact that could be saved from the high universalist conception of the Middle Ages. But this result would have been now acceptable to the world generally if heed had been given to the minority, which, during the thirty years from Arias Montano to the licenciate Valcárcel, clamoured for a strongly Catholic Spain, but a tolerant one. The minority considered that the religious war was a mistake, for it placed Spain in a critical situation with regard to her enemies and kept her deprived of strong allies, who would have prevented the animosity against the power of Spain from becoming, as it did, general throughout the world.

But the isolationism of Spain was not based upon this question of high politico-religious ideals alone. It was also believed that dealing with foreign countries was prejudicial from an economic point of view. The 'Eulogies' of Spain which were written from time to time ever since ancient days had convinced the Spaniards that Spain was an exceptionally rich country, and as it was so, its inhabitants did not need to busy themselves in industry as foreigners did in their more sterile lands. This note of exaggerated optimism, which was already rife in the Middle Ages, still prevailed in the psychology of the Counter-Reformation. The topic of Spain's fertile soil was brilliantly developed by Mendez Silva, by Mariana, by Fray Benito Peñalosa, by Juan Manuel de la Parra, by all in fact, in terms that make Saint Isidore's famous Hymn of Praise seem tame by comparison. Spain is self-sufficient, Spain can satisfy her own needs, and far from needing foreigners, she actually finds them a disturbance. Quevedo considered that Spain was the prey of foreigners, who, on account of the poverty and bleakness of their lands, came to Spain to enrich themselves with the rewards they earned by their industry.

Gracián in his *'Criticón'* resolutely asserts the advantages to be obtained by isolation. In this sense Critilo answers the observation of Andrenio: 'Spain is far apart from the trade of the other provinces and at the end of the world,' with the retort: 'It should be still farther away, for all come in search for it and swallow all the best things it produces: England its generous wines, Holland its soft wool, Venice its glass, Germany its saffron, Naples its silks, Genoa its sugar, France its horses and the whole world its doubloons.'

When we admit this spirit of isolation, this reluctance to having dealings abroad, how can we explain the cultural greatness of Spain in the golden centuries? We must realize that this withdrawal from the rest of Europe, no matter how active it was, only existed in matters that touched high politics and religion, while in the general sphere of culture the isolating tendency did not prevail until a late period. Spain was the chosen people among all others for the defence of religion, and she might live apart in splendid isolation. Her pride and satisfaction was well expressed by the ambassador Mendoza: 'God is powerful in heaven, and the King of Spain on earth'. But beneath this splendid arrogance there was another contrary feeling, excessive too, of over-valuing other peoples who led a kind of life which was less austere than that of the Spaniard. This feeling is noted frequently in the literature of the period and confirmed by Ambrosio de Morales at the time of greatest political power, about 1570. He says: 'We Spaniards of this age have a strange loathing against our own products: we scorn them as if they were the poorest and meanest in the universe and we set the highest value on foreign languages, clothes, victuals, usages and customs.' This discontent Gracián shows again in the same dialogue of Critilo and Andrenio when he says that when they begin to speak ill of Spain they do so feeling sure that Spaniards will not consider it a crime. 'They are not,' he says, 'as suspicious as the French; they are more kindhearted; they embrace all foreigners but they do not value their own people; they are not great admirers of their own country.' This means that the free and open criticism of their own country and the feeling of dissatisfaction, which seemed a novelty peculiar to the eighteenth and nineteenth centuries, already existed in the sixteenth and seventeenth centuries, and it is to be hoped that this frame of mind will never disappear altogether, for it is the most potent force against isolationism. Although Philip II closed the doors and windows of the universities, and although Spain believed itself to be a people set aside by God for His service, this was counteracted by the Spaniards themselves who spread over all Europe, exercising their own fruitful powers of self-criticism. The Spain which, according to Morales, appreciates foreign languages and customs, or embraces all foreigners, according to Gracián, prevails and expresses its own soul tempered by communion with other peoples. The culture of Spain continues its greatness, because when Valdés and Garcilaso led the way by their admiration of Italy they did so with a profound Hispanic consciousness; Ignatius de Loyola, after studying at Alcalá, went to Paris to make himself universal-minded; Lope de Vega, although he felt 'genuinely Spanish' in body and soul, yet sought eagerly the approbation of the Italian and French humanists; Mariana refused to shut himself up in a blind, enthusiastic Hispanism, but demonstrating the truth of the Spanish characteristic noted by Gracián, earned the reproof of having too little enthusiasm for his own country. Finally, the authentic Spain did not shut herself in, but rather broke out of her isolationism, and in every true Spaniard we find the traditional spirit and the spirit of innovation working together in perfect harmony, producing both the mediaeval and those late-maturing fruits in which the mediaeval mingles with the modern.

QUOMODO SEDET SOLA!

The deterioration increased and the policy of isolation produced grave consequences, for it was now regarded as Spain's destiny, accepted proudly but sadly as a legacy inherited from the glories of the past.

In 1609 Quevedo, with the words from Jeremiah, '*Quomodo sedet sola!*' ringing in his heart, opened his tract '*España Defendida*' with a motto in the style of the prophet: 'All our foes opened their mouths against us.' He sees Spain a victim of 'a stubborn persecution', and the Spaniards 'hated by all nations, for all the world is for them a prison and a punishment'; but in spite of all, solitude is steadfastly to be desired, for Spain receives all evil through her communication with foreign peoples; she would not know what excesses in eating and drinking were if the Germans had not introduced them, nor unnatural vice had not Italy taught it to her, nor would the Inquisition have anything to do had Melanchthon, Calvin or Luther never existed. Nevertheless, in spite of these assertions, the sense of solitude becomes embittered, for the disillusion of the extremist Spain of Philip II still lies over the country like a pall of lead. Quevedo thinks that the God of armies helped Spain in the battles of the Cid, at Navas de Tolosa, in the enterprises of Vasco da Gama and Cortés, in the achievements of Cisneros who halted the course of the sun at the taking of Oran, but that golden age is now a thing of the past. Spaniards no longer wear iron armour unless it be to deck the statue on their tomb; they dress in effeminate luxury, 'repenting that they had been begotten men'. On all sides are to be seen insolent married women who boast of their adulteries and men who find the bond of marriage to be a lucrative one. And so when Quevedo in this doctrinal pamphlet remembers from time to time his satirical vein he gives us a very valuable historical commentary on his own burlesque works. The vices against which he there fulminates are not mere defects of normal society deformed and exaggerated in order to produce literary effect, but they are, as it were, a fetid swamp in which the clear stream of a glorious past has lost itself, a past that is still close enough to create all the greater sense of affliction at its loss. Those vices are a sorrowful proof of the corruption which has taken the place of the virtues which have recently vanished together with the spiritual qualities which inspired the creation of the Spanish Empire.

Quevedo, who was the echo of isolationist Spain which was beginning to sink into disillusion, believed that the cause of so great a decline was the peace which the nation enjoyed. 'Although in my opinion,' he says, 'Spain never enjoys peace, she only rests as now from the fatigues of arms, in order to return to the fight with strength unimpaired and fresh courage' against Turks, against heretics and against idolaters of the Indies. In this sense and with this hope Quevedo moderates his pessimism, although peace, namely the peace with Holland, had only been running for very few months, too short a time in which to produce such deep decadence. But in the end wars will start again and the ancient vigorous qualities will return, enabling Spain to carry on her Catholic destiny which is perpetual and immovable. Quevedo in 'Spain Defended', argues about isolation and war, like the majority of his fellow citizens. He reasons from abstract political ideas without paying heed to the inexorable realities.

Twenty years later, the hard reality became only too evident. An obscure Benedictine, Fray Benito de Peñalosa, wrote the truest description of the extreme exaltation which led Spain to wear herself out in her task, accepting with resignation all the poverty which accompanied her greatness. This is clear from the title of the book, which is: 'Book of the five excellences of the Spaniards which depopulate Spain for its greater power and expansion' (*Libro de las cinco excelencias del español que despueblan a España para su mayor potencia y dilatación*, 1629). These 'excellences' are: religion propagated and defended all over the world, the great abundance of theologians and jurists, the arms that have won the greatest empire ever known by man, the nobility with its unevenly distributed privileges, and American gold which has been spent prodigally. Effectively Spain suffers from her own excellences: she is great in purpose and in deeds, but insensitive to her own injuries; and being without the necessary flexibility to adapt herself to changing times and peoples she remains immovable in her isolation from all countries.

But the dangers of such a situation became evident. Quevedo denounced the risks of isolation when he introduced the concept of 'solitude' into the adaptation he made of a saying of Seneca:

> *Y es más fácil, oh España, en muchos modos*
> *que lo que a todos les quitaste sola*
> *te puedan a ti sola quitar todos*
> ('Tis easier, O Spain, in many ways
> for all to take from thee alone
> what thou alone didst take from all).

Years afterwards Quevedo sees that already the enemies are beginning to take away from Spain her prizes. He sees that the Spanish empire not only weakens in her basic ideals, as he had been aware before, but also her material strength was mouldering away. The wars have returned, certainly, in great numbers, but they were unsuccessful wars leading up to the national

misfortunes of Catalonia,[1] Roussillon, Portugal[2] and Recroy.[3]
Quevedo in 1645, eighteen days before his death, relieved his
feelings in a letter to Francisco de Oviedo, saying: 'From all sides
come very bad news of utter ruin, and the worst of it all is that
every one expected this would happen. Señor Don Francisco, I
do not know whether the end is coming or whether 'tis already
come. God only knows; for there are many things which seem
to exist and have their being, and yet they are nought but a word
or a figure.' Quevedo had lost altogether that steadfastness and
that belief in the future which had sustained him in the days when
he wrote 'Spain Defended', and when he believed that the
'modesty, virtue and Christianity' of Philip III, once the war
activity of Spain should begin again, were sufficient to save the
country from the decadence that was descending upon it.

So great, however, was the old belief that Spain was the chosen
people, set apart by God for the purpose of battling for the
Catholic unity of Europe, so vast still was the power of the nation
in both hemispheres, so brilliant also was the cultural activity
that flourished during the centuries of expansion and growth; so
much, too, had been achieved, in spite of the final adversity, that
there was no possibility for the dissenting party in Spain to make
full use of its dissent and secure an entry into the new vital currents of Europe. Would it have still been possible to turn the
national activity of the country in a new direction? Would this
have saved the country? Even though Spain had already lost all
hopes in the possibility of success for her ancient policy yet she
preferred to slumber on in that policy, without the strength to
create new national projects in accordance with the new times
which the progress of the different peoples had brought to Europe.

INNOVATING SPAIN COMES INTO ACTION

The isolationist spirit met with strong resistance from the
moment of the War of Succession. The two aspects of abnormal

[1] The rebellion of Catalonia in 1640–1652 to hand the province to Louis XIII of
France; Roussillon, which was acquired by Ferdinand the Catholic in 1493,
rebelled with Catalonia in 1640 and remained in the power of Louis XIII.

[2] Portugal was incorporated in the dominions of Philip II in 1580 and became
independent in 1640.

[3] Rocroy, town in the Ardennes where the Conde de Fuentes was defeated on
19 May 1643. This marked the end of the military supremacy of the Spanish
Infantry.

violence which we noted in other outstanding periods (Alfonso VI and Charles V) were bound to reappear again at this time. On the one hand the invasion of foreigners occurred owing to the fact that the armies of France, England and Austria fought on Spanish soil during the first fourteen years of the eighteenth century, followed by the arrival of a host of ministers, courtiers, technicians, either Italian or French, who under the new dynasty of the Bourbons took part in the Government and the life of Spain. Then on the other hand the uprooting of traditional ideas and usages frequently was carried out in an authoritarian manner, by means of government decrees which aroused discontent, protests and even riots. All the forces of innovation, if they did not level the traditional walls of isolationism, yet breached it in many places and allowed in many influences from outside. Spain now found that the great events of history had definitely decided against her, for a new concept of public life had grown up in the two countries that had been her bitterest enemies, namely England and Holland, and had spread throughout Europe. The religious question, which had caused the shedding of so much blood in the two preceding centuries, could not be solved on the field of battle or by state compulsion, and so was to be left to the inviolable sanctuary of the individual conscience. The State aimed exclusively at dealing with the problems concerning material and intellectual culture. In this field of action the backwardness of Spain in comparison to other countries, owing to its isolated life, was enormous. This was noticed by many Spaniards who were discontented with the past, and this section of public opinion, which in former days had been unable to give voice to its views, now found support in the actions of the State which had been inspired by the new dynasty to introduce a progressive policy.

But now, from the beginning of the eighteenth century, the spiritual unity of the Spaniards, which during the two previous centuries had appeared to the external world to be strong and unbroken, with the exception of small and accidental schisms, shows the deep antagonism caused by two ideologies which frequently reached a climax of exaltation. The points of divergence might vary according to the times, but in the end the struggle was always for religious motives. When the mediaeval toleration began to be restricted by the Catholic monarchs, intolerance was necessary for a meritorious purpose, namely that of achieving the necessary national unity, so that the Spanish people might launch out into great external enterprises. Now, in modern days, when national unification was not possible under that militant spirit of Catholicism, which at the time of the European struggle had been so highly successful as a unifying force, an intolerant zeal lasted on throughout half the country, wrecking by its ceaseless antagonism all the benefits of unity which had been achieved in the past. It is not that the anti-Catholics were numerous; they were in fact very few. But the intolerant anti-Progressives looked upon any one who proposed new-fangled notions as a downright enemy, even though those ideas were in no way a danger to religion. And vice versa, out-and-out modernizers pushed on their schemes without any regard for religious interests.

From the beginning an attempt was made to put Spain into intellectual communication with the European countries from which for two centuries she had tried to isolate herself. Feijóo[1] laments the exclusiveness of both sides; on the one side are those whom he calls *nacionistas*, which is the same as 'antinationals' for they admire in unmeasured fashion foreign nations and everything in their own country seems to them uncouth and barbarous. On the opposite side are those who believe that their land contains all the treasures and virtues that are to be found in the world, and they look down with scorn upon the other nations, making fun of their advances in arts and sciences, for they believe that foreign books bring nothing new save futile frivolities. Feijóo takes up his position between one party and the other, but owing to the exigencies of the times he found it much more necessary to incline to the side of the innovators in order to combat ceaselessly the prejudices, superstitions and the backwardness of the isolationists. These declared themselves the sworn enemies of all that was done or thought by the 'foreigners, who are either heretics or well on the way to be so', and so they wished to close all entrance to what they called 'the infected air of the north'—a

[1] Fray Benito Jerónimo Feijóo (1676–1764), Benedictine, represents in Spain the new ideas of the eighteenth century which he set forth in his *Teatro crítico universal*, eight volumes, 1726-1737, and his *Cartas eruditas y curiosas*, five volumes, and various other works. Consult *Las ideas biológicas del Padre Feijóo*, by Gregorio Marañón, second edition 1941.

phrase, added Feijóo, 'which became the stock one in such matters, and a most efficacious method for hallucinating many good
Catholics, but as ignorant as they are Catholic.' These ignorant
people, in great alarm, insistently opposed the valiant Benedictine, but Ferdinand VI gave him his protection and prevented
them from attacking him (1750). Feijóo achieved lasting fame
and his success was due to his moderation and his comprehensive
judgement. 'No other Spaniard,' says Marañón justly, 'did as
much as Feijóo to incorporate our soul in the soul of the world
without tarnishing its traditional innocence. He felt the longing
for renovation that was characteristic of his century without
destroying a single one of the roots of his national tradition.'

Nevertheless the secularizing policy of the Bourbons did not
bring so complete a change as is generally believed, for it did not
by any means favour modernism at any price. The new kings,
although they did not put religion before anything else and
allow it to guide their actions as the Austrian monarchy did,
yet always allied themselves strictly with the Catholic feeling in
the country. The ministers of the government used to pay attention to the fears and misgivings of the traditional extremists and
often supported them by linking them with their own political
suspicions. As a result they often looked askance at authentic
innovations, no matter how much these may have respected the
rooted beliefs and customs of the nation. The government supported the ideas of 'Enlightenment' and 'Progress', which were
inspired by the French, and also the sciences, arts, and industries;
in order to make up for two centuries of isolation they brought in
foreign technicians, and they sent young Spaniards to study
abroad. But they always acted with the utmost caution for fear
lest some danger from an intellectual source, no matter how
remote or fictitious it might be, would imperil the monarchical or
religious system. For this reason the Inquisition and the strict
civil censorship still continued functioning. All this policy of
limitation was necessary at the beginning, in the interests of
prudence, but afterwards it was carried on too long.

Two representative names will enable us to understand the
difference between the 'Enlightenment' of the authorities and
that of the truly independent spirits, no matter how moderate
and prudent they were. Forner, who had been educated at the

University of Salamanca, was, in accordance with the spirit of
that centre of learning, a 'scholastic' or a 'peripatetic' as the
phrase went there, or a 'Gothic' as such students were nicknamed. He spoke with scorn of Descartes, Leibnitz and Newton
and praised only the sciences reputed to be 'useful to mankind',
namely theology, moral philosophy, jurisprudence and medicine. He defended passionately government censorship and isolationism, for he believed that Spanish libraries were none the
poorer because in them were not to be found Rousseau, Helvetius,
Bayle, Voltaire, and a host of other authors of disquisitions on
useless and frivolous subjects (the futilities of foreign books,
according to the isolationists censured by Feijóo). Against
Forner, Cadalso took up the cudgels on behalf of the 'modernists'
or *ilustrados*, for he believed that scholasticism and Aristotelian-
ism, which his opponents considered to be as sacred and eternal
as religion itself, were upheld only from sheer mental laziness.
For this reason he encouraged those students who studied
secretly the positive sciences 'in order that they might not be
called barbarians by the foreign students'; and it was to be hoped
that in a few years the whole scientific system of Spain would
change as a result of the study of forbidden books in which the
students would discover 'a thousand truths not in any way
opposed to religion or fatherland but only to idleness and prejudice'. As this reading and writing had to be done in secret,
Cadalso could not utter such opinions in public. He wrote
sorrowfully to Iriarte that in opposition to the ignorant people
who believe Spain to be the best country in the world, there are
those who see the evils and know the remedy for them, but they
have to retire into some corner, for those who speak out are made
to keep silence. And the two statesmen, Aranda and Florida-
blanca, who were considered advanced Voltairians, were the
very persons who ordered Cadalso to keep silence and not to publish the 'Moroccan Letters' and to limit himself to being 'exclusively military'. On the other hand they encouraged Forner
to publish his '*Apologia*' (1786) wherein he shows himself to be
Aristotelian and 'Gothic'. This shows plainly the cautious
limitation of government reforms. Even the idea of the utilitarian
value of intellectual culture remains unaltered. The only activities of the intellect which bring immediate profit to man as

enumerated by Forner are those described by Quevedo as 'solid sciences', opposed to other lucubrations of the intellect which are superfluous, vain and harmful. Thus on this occasion as well as formerly there is the same misgiving about pure science, which must be studied secretly, as Cadalso said.

The Cadalso thus condemned to work in silence was in reality a moderate man well-balanced in everything and always maintaining his position between the two opposing tendencies. On the one hand he censured those who would live only according to the customs and thoughts of former days, that is to say in the ancient Spanish manner, and he proves to such people that they are unable to understand the 'genuine national qualities'. Something they appreciate as being most Spanish, the costume of the day, was a novelty that dated only from the Austrian dynasty. On the other hand he is more severe in his criticisms of the opposite exaggerations, and he especially attacks those who believe that they are distilling the quintessence of modernism when they speak badly of their country and listen joyfully to foreigners who satirize her, from the hairdresser and the dancing-master upwards; he ridicules the young lady who is inconsolable in Madrid, who is 'ashamed of being Spanish', and all this because she cannot find in the shops of the capital a ribbon of the colour she wanted.

In spite of the fact that the authorities with their extremely limited sense of modern life promoted the work of Forner and prohibited that of Cadalso, though there was no very deep change in the scope of cultural life, yet there did take place a change on the practical side. When the practical concerns of the State, so long neglected, received full recognition, innovating Spain made some advance after its long period of inactivity. The first mutual concessions which were made between the two opposing tendencies opened a period of considerable advance, the most outstanding of modern times, which culminates in the reigns of Ferdinand VI and Charles III.

This movement, though basically moderate, as it was an unfamiliar novelty after the long preceding period of weakness, seemed to its opponents to be excessive, and even the ultra-conservatives of to-day consider it exaggerated. Doubtless there were excesses, some of them of regrettable violence, such as the expulsion of the Jesuits, but the general idea of the reform was

moderate. Nevertheless, as the collision between the two antagonistic forces, which formerly had been hardly perceptible, now
became apparent and even acquired unusually high relief, it
seems as if the schism between the two Spains took place for the
first time in the eighteenth century. There is no doubt that it was
one of the strongest and most definite cleavages, for to find
another as deep and tumultuous we should probably have to go
back to the eleventh century.

So strange does the innovation introduced in the eighteenth
century appear that it affects our whole assessment of the national
life. Most marked is the concept of 'decadence' envisaged from
two opposite viewpoints. Modernists like Cadalso believed that
the prosperous period ended with the Catholic monarchs. After
them began a long period of decline. The policy of Philip II exhausted the strength of the country to no purpose and left Spain
completely ruined materially and two centuries behind the rest
of Europe. These arrears have to be made up urgently, by shaking
the country out of its apathetic stagnation. On the other side the
traditionalists denied this idea of decline; they considered that
the reign of Philip II and the action of the Counter-Reformation
were the zenith of Spain's glory, and they held that this action
must be maintained and continued in spite of its defeat in the
international political field, at least as an internal rule of conduct. In this way the nation would save, at any rate, the pure
essence of Spain, with the contamination of which by the corruption of modern European civilization there had set in a fatal
disorder which it was necessary to check.

The opposition of Spain to Europe during the time of the
Counter-Reformation had now been transferred to within the
country itself, and we find a purist Spain facing a Europeanizing
Spain, two halves that cannot easily reach any mutual agreement
which will ensure harmonious and continued action. The men
who were most capable of creating this harmonious action, such
as Cadalso, were unable to exercise any decisive influence. Later
on Jovellanos,[1] a man whose new ideas of the 'Enlightenment'

---

[1] Gaspar Melchor de Jovellanos (1744–1811), in the transition between the
eighteenth and nineteenth centuries, is the principal writer on social, economic
and political questions. He was also a lyric, didactic, and dramatic poet. He was
exiled from 1790 to 1797 and was again exiled in 1798 and a prisoner between
1801 and 1808.

were balanced by a deep love for his country, and a genuine respect for the history of Spain, one therefore who stood for harmony between the two antagonistic Spains, and could have inspired a truly progressive movement of deep significance, had no political power at his disposal and was in fact repeatedly persecuted by the state authorities.

THE TWO SPAINS IN CIVIL WAR

The Napoleonic war enabled progressive Spain, hitherto rather timid, to realize that she had come of age; and now that she was released from the trammels of absolute monarchy, she could, for the first time, hold advanced political opinions, thus intensifying the opposition between contrary ideologies. The struggle which had declared itself all over Europe between revolution and tradition now broke out in Spain with the greatest violence. On the one hand the Constitution of Cadiz, as radical as that of any other nation, suddenly introduced very advanced reforms and contemptuously overwhelmed the deeply-rooted conservative spirit of the country; on the other hand the reaction when it came cancelled with a stroke of the pen all that had been done, as though nothing had happened since Charles IV, as if the people had not lived in a few years a period of deliverance from worn-out notions.

More than ever half of Spain denied the other half. The Constitutionalists of Cadiz did not try for a single moment to limit their aspirations by considering what was the force represented by their opponents; they considered the force as non-existent. Likewise the reactionaries thought that nothing in the Constitution was worthy of respect, and they, too, imagined that the Constitutionalists were of no account in the country; they were only a set of reprobates worthy to be chastised by the Angel of Extermination, both themselves and 'their families even to the fourth generation'. And when the Extermination by Ferdinand VII came, it was carried out in such an implacable way that it frightened the very foreigners who were intervening in favour of Ferdinand VII, such as the Duke of Angoulême, the enthusiastic Catholic and lover of Spain Chateaubriand, Louis XVIII, all those, in fact, who were in vain trying to make the absolutists come to some kind of harmonious agreement with the liberals.

Shortly after came the final consequence of extremist opinions, namely civil war, which is always apparently either a war of succession or secession, but one which never ends, even though blood ceases to be shed after the peace has been made. All the forces of the nation were engaged in an exhausting struggle on behalf of insoluble problems concerning the practice of state activity, and forgot the urgent collective enterprises which must be accomplished if life in common is to have any meaning. The two Spains while fighting for the highest principles neglected all the immediate aims, namely those essential to their life in common.

Larra in '*El día de difuntos de 1836*' ('All Souls' Day 1836') seeing the Carlist war extend all over Spain, and remembering the rising of the sergeants of 1812 against the monarchy and many other bitter struggles, finds nothing but death and tombs on one side as well as on the other: '*Here lies the Inquisition; it died of old age*'; '*Here rests freedom of thought; died in infancy*'; '*Here lies military discipline*'; '*Here rests Spanish credit*'; and finally the most depressing epitaph of all: '*Here lies half Spain, it died at the hands of the other half.*'

And so the mortal duel between the two halves continued like a horrible nightmare. Already traditional Spain appeared to be dead, and a French traveller (Théophile Gautier), when noting the irreverent behaviour of the Madrid populace during the procession of Corpus Christi in 1840, and the emptiness of Seville Cathedral, now only visited by occasional tourists, concludes: 'Spain is no longer Catholic.' But then (1842) when Balmes asked himself anxiously: 'Is it true that Spain is still Catholic?' he could answer hopefully: Catholicism is the strongest regenerative force that the Spanish nation possesses. This took place under the banner of Espartero. Soon afterwards under the opposite banner of Narváez, liberal Spain was, in theory, condemned to sterility and death, when Donoso Cortés, who had recently been converted from liberalism (1848), urged on by the exaggeration which he himself confessed was the 'historical characteristic of Spaniards', denied to his former liberal colleagues even the smallest capacity for good. His infallible political axiom, following the traditionalism of Bonald, was that nothing which did not follow the dictates of Catholicism could be acceptable, seeing that human reason always produces evil unmixed with good and follows error as a mother follows her child.

And this exclusive idea, whether expressed as here in the form of a definite system, and as such disapproved by the Church, or whether believed unconsciously and practised diligently, was the guiding-force of the Spanish right-wing thinkers.[1] In vain were voices raised in favour of a more moderate policy. Balmes once, in 1845, under the same banner of Narváez uttered the warning that it was necessary to pay some attention to the 'new Spain that imitates the foreigner'; it was a wise policy to offer ways and means whereby it might reform and evolve, 'for we must not count too much upon repressive measures.' But Balmes decided to keep silent, for he found himself derided by the ultra right-wing extremists as a liberal cleric, a Spanish Lamennais. Even Pope Pius IX, whom Balmes so much admired, was called 'the liberal pope' by these extremists of the right-wing.

This extremist policy continued inexorably. Menéndez Pelayo, even in the early years when he was rigidly right-wing (1877), was accused of being lukewarm by the ultra-Catholics, disciples of Donoso Cortés. On the opposite side those who kept repeating that 'Spain is no longer Catholic' were legion. And so the struggle continued without any attempt being made by either side to understand the other. Governments formed from both sides followed one another, lasting two, four or six years, but rarely longer. Generally the periods of right-wing rule lasted longer as such governments were more determined and unified in their views, but all the time there was the same mutual intolerance which sent the ship of state tossing from side to side, never allowing it to follow a fixed course.

OPPOSING CONCEPTS OF HISTORY

The concept of history that belongs to each of the two ideologies spreads deeper and wider in the nineteenth than in the eighteenth century. It continues to pivot on the period of greatest prosperity reached by the nation and the subsequent

[1] For lack of any better terms, I use these old parliamentary expressions of right and left, which by their vagueness have varied greatly in meaning at different periods. (Author's note).

decline. This theme of decline became an obsession entailing two questions; first of all: When did this decline begin? or to put it another way, What is the historical character of the events which determined the decline? Secondly: What consequences ensue for the present as a result of the events which ended the preceding state of prosperity?

The traditionalist thinkers approved totally the part played by Spain in the sixteenth and seventeenth centuries, for it was then that the nation reached its zenith of power and glory, and produced the most brilliant examples of her activity in all walks of life. The thought and action developed in that golden age were essentially true to the Spanish genius and should be taken as a programme that Spain should follow always, unless she wishes to renounce her essential spirit. The decline developed as a result of having abandoned the guiding force that operated in those golden centuries. Menéndez Pelayo believes that this unfortunate abandonment began with the expulsion of the Jesuits or perhaps in the last decade of the eighteenth century, that is to say at the time when Charles IV held his Voltairian court, and the 'Encyclopédie' was the order of the day. Maeztu,[1] who was more particularly concerned with isolationism, considers that the change in ideas took place a little earlier, about 1750, when the Marquis de la Ensenada was already in power; he it was who invented scholarships for study abroad which were responsible for the introduction into the Peninsula of the spirit of foreign peoples. This was for Maeztu indeed an evil day, for if in former centuries Spain had too much neglected material interests and science, on the other hand, it must be recognized that while the Europe of Galileo and Descartes was creating modern science with its more positive results, Spain kept its *Philosophia perennis*, which was the most valuable of all knowledge. The result, therefore, of the sinister change which took place in intellectual and religious matters was that Spain interrupted its true history in order to imitate France, and for the past 200 years she has been losing her soul in the effort to be what she is not.

To these views the anti-isolationist thinkers reply that the material and scientific backwardness of the country recognized

[1] Ramiro de Maeztu (1875–1936), journalist, essayist and principal exponent of the *Hispanidad* movement in his *Defensa de la Hispanidad*, 1934.

by both sides is a proof that Spain cannot be in the right against all the other countries. They believed, as did Cadalso, that Spain abandoned its true course, not in the eighteenth but in the sixteenth century, when she took up a position of isolation in Europe, and was left behind culturally. Costa indeed holds that real Spain ends with the death of Cisneros. Every good liberal of the last century thought that Charles V, when he crushed the Communes, acted as a bloodthirsty despot. Following this line Macías Picavea considered the Austrian dynasty to be a foreign body which, when grafted on to the Spanish people, paralysed its natural evolution. Everything that happened afterwards was a disaster, says Castelar in his rhetorical manner, and nothing is more lamentable than that great Spanish Empire stretched out over the planet like a vast shroud. Thus was denied the essential and permanent identity between the ideals of the two golden centuries and the spirit of the Spanish people, and this negation was upheld by well-known writers in different fields of knowledge who cover the last quarter of the nineteenth and the beginning of the twentieth century. The oldest of those writers, Juan Valera, directs his arguments in 1876 against those who considered that for Spain to recover her lost prosperity it would be necessary to return to a social, political and religious state similar to that of the sixteenth century. Such people, he thought, did not take into account the inevitable evolution of human affairs. What produced that greatness in former ages cannot produce it now, and it would be necessary to demonstrate whether those ideas and customs of the past were the cause of the greatness or whether they were the cause of the corruption and rapid decline, for there is no doubt that the infirmity leading to decline under the Austrian kings was overweening pride, a belief that, like the Jews, they were the chosen people, and it was this obsession which estranged Spain from the rest of Europe. Later came other thinkers, who, while considering the link with the past necessary, sought for the true Spanish tradition not in its particular manifestations in the golden centuries but in the innermost recesses of the people's soul, the rock foundations on which alone can any true structure be built up. To this belief were due works such as those of Costa concerning primitive customs and the politico-legal significance of mediaeval popular poetry, and also the tendency to encourage youth to travel and acquire an intimate knowledge of their fatherland not only in its present, but in its past by studying its archaeology, history, landscapes, geology, crafts, folk songs and regional customs. It was the same desire to conciliate both the old and the new spirit that made Ganivet say that without doubt it would be necessary to continue the spirit of traditional Spain, but not with the same aims in view, for the motives of the past led Spain to interfere in European affairs, which was 'a monstrous absurdity', whereas if on completing the Reconquest Spain had only concentrated on her internal activity, she might have become a Christian Greece. 'Generally speaking,' says Ganivet, 'tradition, contrary to what is believed, cannot produce an energetic impulse, because in intellectual life the past, although it is powerful as a centre of resistance, is weak as a spur to action.' Unamuno is more categorical, for he considers that Spain by mixing herself up with European affairs contradicted her true nature. He thinks that in order to continue our tradition we do not need to copy the ideas of the past, but to delve into the *intrahistorical* depths of the Spanish people and extract from there the forces which once vitalized those ideas and which may vitalize others, for what is 'eternal' in the spirit of the people will survive only on condition that what is 'historical' is forgotten.

This manner of considering tradition not as an immediate and invariable mentor but as an inspiration, correct though it be, is not easily understood by everybody, and all that the majority generally extract from the doctrine is a scornful rejection of the sixteenth and seventeenth centuries, without discovering any positive values to take their place, so that this rejection is equivalent to a denationalization. In spite of Costa, Ganivet or Unamuno, the left-wing parties were very little inclined to study and point out in historical traditions any aspects that coincided with their own ideology; they were never interested in selecting a traditional idea which tallied with any of the basic principles of liberalism; they only remembered the 'monstrous absurdity', the 'shroud extended over the planet'; they generally saw in the sixteenth century only what they considered to be inapplicable to the present, and they failed to see that essential and enduring historical element, which can always be reassimilated and is fertile for ever. The quest for what is eternally pure and genuine does not mean, as Unamuno insists, that one should forget historical tradition, for there is no opposition, since this 'eternal' spirit underlies all history. It betrays lack of understanding not to appreciate in Spanish history the noble and fruitful part played by the country in the sixteenth century, wherein the only fault was that Spain did not evolve in accordance with the unescapable necessities of modern life. In the antagonism between the two Spains this historical pessimism was a definite sign of the inferiority of the left-wing parties. Urged on by their intolerant party feeling they abandoned all the strength of tradition to their enemies, and allowed their right-wing opponents to win entire profit from the solid support of Menéndez Pelayo who with unmatched art and learning exalted all our bygone history, calling it a glory of the past and a guide to the future.

But Menéndez Pelayo, though in mature years he rectified the extremist views of his youthful polemical writings, and though no one better than he could have achieved the conciliation of the two antagonistic groups, did not succeed in doing so. He saw that the adverse historical judgement of the left-wing party was gaining ground owing to the state of mind created by the disaster of 1898. He saw a continual increase among the intellectuals of this tendency to reject the past, and at the end of his life he became bitterly pessimistic as he watched 'the long, slow suicide of a people, who, deceived by garrulous sophists, grimly liquidates its own past, makes mock of its ancestors, and rejects all that in History made them great'.

Certainly the mood of general pessimism made those who wished for a renewal of values take a still more gloomy view of Spanish history. Formerly it was admitted that there had been a brilliant period of prosperity followed by a long decline which began, according to some, with Philip II, and according to others, with Charles III or Charles IV; but now a negative pathological note is used to characterize all past history. As early as 1912 and 1913 Azorín severely questioned the prosperity created by the Catholic monarchs, as described by Ganivet, saying: 'Spain has never, even in her most brilliant century, the sixteenth, had a moment of genuine vitality.' In 1920 the Duke of Maura wrote a striking, fully documented work to show that the

capital defects now considered to have been the causes of the
decline could be observed in every period of Spanish history from
Ataulf to to-day. Spain has not been suffering a decline from the
sixteenth century, but ever since the Middle Ages she has been
suffering from 'congenital atrophy of the noblest organ of
national life, namely civic spirit', though this illness is not an irreparable hindrance to great individual actions. About the same
time Ortega Gasset, in a memorable essay of 1921, maintained
with his great authority that Spain has not suffered a decline in
modern days, but has been in bad health ever since the time of
the invasion of the Goths. She suffers from a constitutional
deficiency—the absence, or, at least, the scarcity of directive
minorities capable of leading the masses of the people, and she
also suffers from the fact that the masses in Spain are so refractory
to any discipline. This it is that has produced 'invertebrate
Spain'.

In thus rejecting the idea of decline we are really affirming the
characteristics of the Spanish people which have lasted throughout the centuries. We are inclined to go further back in the study
of basic characteristics, noting them not merely in the days of
Ataulf[1] but even as far back as Indibil[2]; and we should consider
those examples not only from the pathological aspect so dear to
the pessimists of the post-1898 period, but as signs of a vitality
which does not cease to be normal because its defects and qualities do not tally with those of neighbouring countries. With this
idea in view historical works have been written, and we find that
the generation of '98 has co-operated in revaluing the past.
Azorín, always among the leaders, goes as far as denying the
reality of the well-worn theme of historical decline (1924).
Baroja, who had given such impulse to this belief, with his
mournful references to Spain, the Country of Gloom, in 1935,
even if in spite of Menéndez Pelayo's defence he does not think
highly of the achievements of Spanish science, yet considers that
Spanish culture, as a whole, is one of the three or four most

[1] As the allusion to Ataulf, the first Gothic king of Spain in the fifth century,
implies that the characteristics date from the beginning of the Middle Ages, so
the name of Indibil, an Iberian chieftain of the third century B.C., links these
characteristics with the Ancient World.
[2] Indibil was a prince of the tribe of the Ilergetes at the time when the Scipios
began the Roman domination of Spain in the years 212 and 205 B.C.

important in the world. But this new current of understanding, barely initiated, has had no time to produce results.

SPANISH EXCLUSIVENESS RECEIVES INTERNATIONAL SUPPORT

During the first third of the present century the Spanish exclusiveness of the left- and right-wing parties found formidable support in the complex reaction which had taken place in Europe as a result of the crisis of liberalism. This reaction brought in the rule of *the collectivity*, the supremacy of the State, whether communist or nationalist, and the new dictatorial state in Europe would admit no dissenters in its ranks, and only allowed the existence of the so-called 'one party'. The expression itself is a contradiction in terms; a party which wishes to be all and do without the other parties. This exclusive policy fitted in admirably with the usual Spanish intolerance, in fact it strengthened it. It was not enough to refuse to compromise with the antagonistic half of Spain, it was necessary to suppress it totally so as to become all-powerful. The monarchy in its last phase found itself driven to deny with due solemnity the other Spain. This took place on the occasion of the visit of Alfonso XIII to Rome in November 1923. The King in his speech at the Vatican announced to the Pope that Spain to-day continued the Spain of Philip II which battled in the name of the Church: 'If like another Urban II in defence of the persecuted faith you start a new crusade against the enemies of our holy religion, Spain and her king will never desert the place of honour.' The King affirmed the unanimity of the country, saying: 'These are wishes of my whole people,' and he went on to remind His Holiness especially of 'the consecration which at El Cerro de los Angeles, amidst the applause of all my subjects and in presence of my government, I made of Spain to the Most Sacred Heart of Jesus'. But in his reply Pius XI, precisely the Pope who consecrated the world to the Sacred Heart, did not consider it opportune to deny in this way the existence of the problem of the two Spains, and he gave a fatherly warning, reminding the King that among the great and noble Spanish people 'there are also unhappy children of ours, though still most beloved of us, who refuse to draw near to the

Divine Heart; tell them that we do not exclude them on that account from our prayers and blessings, but, on the contrary, our thoughts go out to them, and our love.' Thus the Pope, even on this occasion of diplomatic courtesy, did not refrain from denouncing and correcting as a political error the affirmation of a single Spain, ready to crusade as a 'chosen people of Providence', as the king's speech put it. He did not offer one word of thanks for the suggested crusade, but on the contrary, he gave warning that the Spain which did not conform to those views should be borne in mind. What a catastrophe, and what a deluge of blood would have been avoided if both sides, instead of denying the existence of the opposing Spain, had recognized it mutually and tried to win it over by genuine affection, as Pius XI did, recognizing it as an inevitable fact which needed charity and comprehension.

The right-wing partisans continued to look upon those who were in dissent not as an integral sector of the nation, but as its enemies. They called the opposite side 'anti-Spain' and 'anti-fatherland', in imitation of the 'anti-France' used by Charles Maurras, and the 'anti-Italy' used by Marinetti. But in Spain this word 'anti' was applied to everybody, no matter how patriotic he was, if he did not unconditionally belong to the ultra-right-wing party. The left-wing parties, likewise, felt the same determination to suppress their adversaries. They, through the voice of Azaña, proclaimed that Catholic Spain had ceased to exist on the exact day, the twelfth of April 1931, when the republicans triumphed in the elections. They alone were the fatherland; their opponents were a set of despicable cave-dwellers, and if the latter on their side thought it necessary to suppress the eighteenth and nineteenth centuries, the triumphant republicans declared that the history of Spain had been a mistake from the days of the conversion.

ONE SPAIN

Larra lamented over half Spain as dead, yet the deceased rose from the tomb to continue the mortal struggle. A hundred years later, when Azaña proclaimed the death of Catholic Spain, the latter rose and it was republican Spain which fell. This was the fated destiny of the two sons of Oedipus, who would not consent to reign together and mortally wounded each other. Will this sinister craving to destroy the adversary ever cease? Evil days indeed have come upon the world when extremism of a kind that leaves that of Spain far behind appears on all sides, and when a ferocious cleavage such as had never before existed makes national life in common impossible in many countries, owing to the mad exclusive tendencies which have gripped the dominant parties in the state. Mussolini called the twentieth century the era of collectivity, the century of the State; but for Italy and Germany this century lasted only a couple of decades, and we do not yet know how the democracies will fare after the victory which they share with communism. Nevertheless, in spite of the all-powerful collectivism which has achieved its unanimity only at the cost of a ruthless and exclusive policy, the individual will again win back his rights, which allow him to disagree, to rectify and invent afresh, for it is to the individual that we owe all the great deeds of history.

To suppress those who think differently and crush projects for what our brothers believe to be a better life, is to sin against prudence. And even in questions where one side sees itself in possession of the absolute truth as against the error of the other side, it is not right to smother all manifestations of error (as it is impossible to suppress the side itself), for then we should reach the demoralizing situation of living without an opposition, and there is no worse enemy than not to have one. There is a great deal of wisdom contained in the humorous wish expressed by Ganivet that Spanish Catholics should remedy their lack of opponents, and bring here some Protestants or heretics on hire, so as to act as a tonic to the Catholicism of the peninsula.

The hard reality of events is bound to strengthen toleration, that priceless fruit of the experience of the noblest peoples, not to be destroyed by the collectivist extremism now spread over the world. It is not one of the half-Spains that will prevail as a single party and write the epitaph of the other half. It will not be a Spain of the right or of the left, but that integral Spain for which so many have longed, the Spain that has not amputated one of her arms, but makes full use of all her capabilities in the laborious task of winning for herself a place among the peoples that give an impulse to modern life. Two organs necessary for existence must enter into function. First, a traditional Spain unshakable in her

Catholicism which, hating violence, not only avoids coercion of the dissident, but shares with them in brotherly fashion the interest taken by the State in the common welfare; thus offering to the innovators, as Balmes suggested, possibilities of evolution and reform. Secondly, a new Spain, full of the spirit of modernity, non-isolationist, interested in foreign standards but not idly subject to them: her originality rooted, as Unamuno said, in the 'eternal', not in the 'historic'. She will look on the past achievement of her people not, as did Castelar, under the similitude of a funeral shroud, nor with merely cold respect, but with affectionate interest in that Spain of old which shed such brilliance on important periods of universal history.

The sorrows of Spain, one and eternal, deeply felt by all who in their thoughts on history rise above the dissensions of the past, will bring about the needed reintegration, in spite of the fierce storm of antagonisms that rages in the world. The normalization of our existence demands that every Spaniard, in fruitful sympathy with his brother, should give play within himself to the two tendencies of tradition and renovation, the two forces that produce by their intimate struggle the greatest benefits for humanity; those two souls which Unamuno said he bore within himself, that of a traditionalist and that of a liberal, in unending but fruitful discussion. It was this double impulse which made Menéndez Pelayo at one time exalt the intolerance of sword and bonfire, and later on point out that the truly Christian thing was 'not to kill any one'. This too made him at first despise the literary fame of Galdós and afterwards choose the most solemn occasion to pay him a warm tribute, grieving that he had once attacked him 'with violent anger'. This calm and understanding spirit will make it possible for Spaniards to live in concord on their native soil; not in unanimity, for that is neither possible in a world handed over by God to the disputes of men, nor is it desirable, but at least united for a common Hispanic purpose which inevitably cannot be the same as that which united Spaniards in the Golden Age. If Spaniards can join together for the great collective tasks before them, if they can agree in establishing an era based on justice and selectivity free from party prejudice, they will at last bring to an end these tossings of the ship of State and set her on a steady course towards the high destinies of the nation.

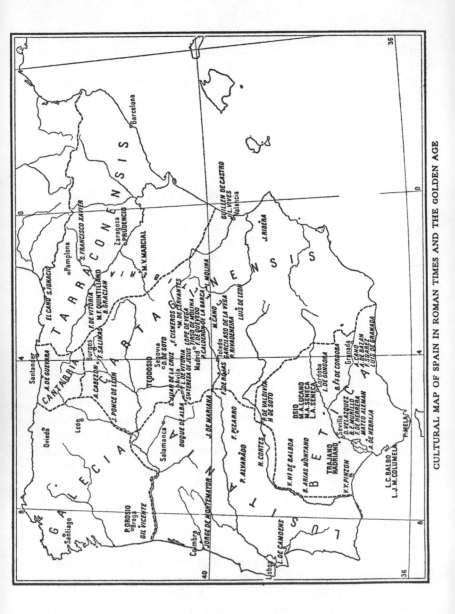

CULTURAL MAP OF SPAIN IN ROMAN TIMES AND THE GOLDEN AGE

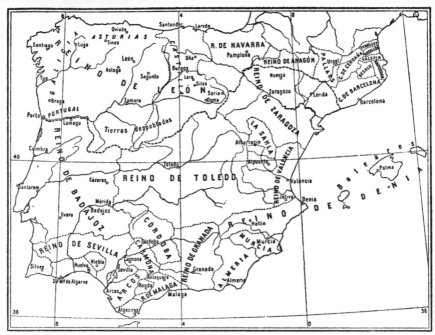

CHRISTIAN AND MOORISH KINGDOMS AT THE MIDDLE OF THE 11th CENTURY

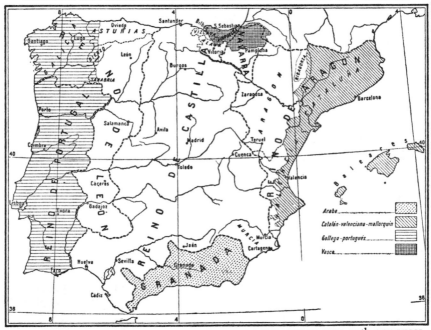

THE MEDIAEVAL KINGDOMS AND DIFFERENT LANGUAGES IN THE 13th CENTURY

BIBLIOGRAPHY

OF THE PRINCIPAL WORKS BY
D. RAMÓN MENÉNDEZ PIDAL

La Leyenda de los Infantes de Lara, Madrid, 1896; 2nd ed. 1934.

Crónicas Generales de España. Catálogo de la Real Biblioteca. Manuscritos, Madrid, 1898.

Notas para el Romancero del Conde Fernán González, Madrid, 1899.

Poema del Cid, Annotated edition, Madrid, 1900.

'El Condenado por Desconfiado', por Tirso de Molina, Madrid, 1902.

La Leyenda del Abad Don Juan de Montemayor, Dresden, 1903.

Manual Elemental de Gramática Histórica Española, Madrid, 1904.

Primera Crónica General de España que mandó componer Alfonso el Sabio y se continuaba bajo Sancho IV en 1289, Madrid, 1906; 2nd ed. 1916.

Cantar de Mío Cid. Text, grammar and vocabulary, Madrid, 1908. Vol. I.

L'Epopée castillane a travers la littérature espagnole, translated by Henry Mérimée, with a preface by Ernest Mérimée, Paris, 1910; 2nd ed. in Spanish, Madrid and Buenos Aires, 1945.

El Romancero Español. Lectures given in Columbia University, New York, on the 5th and 7th of April 1909, under the auspices of the Hispanic Society of America, New York, 1910.

Cantar de Mío Cid. Text, grammar and vocabulary, Madrid, 1911. Vols. II and III.

Poema del Mío Cid. Introduction, text and notes, Madrid, 1913. Ed. La Lectura.

Manual Elemental de Gramática Histórica Española, Madrid, 1914.

La Serrana de la Vera, de Luis Vélez de Guevara, published by R. Menéndez Pidal and María Goyri de Menéndez Pidal, Madrid, 1916.

Antología de Prosistas Castellanos. Madrid, 1917. 3rd ed. 1920.

Manual de Gramática Histórica Española, Madrid, 1918; 4th ed., with corrections and additions.

Documentos Lingüísticos de España—I: "Reino de Castilla", Madrid, 1919.

Estudios Literarios, Madrid, 1920.

Un aspecto en la Elaboración del Quijote, Ateneo de Madrid. (Lecture given at the inauguration of the course, 1920–21, by R. Menéndez Pidal, President of the Ateneo), Madrid, 1920.

Introducción al Estudio de la Lingüística Vasca, in *Cursos de metodología y alta cultura. Curso de lingüística*, Barcelona, 1921.

Poesía Popular y Poesía Tradicional en la Literatura Española, Oxford University Press, 1922.

El Rey Rodrigo en la Literatura, Bulletin of the Royal Spanish Academy, 1924.

Poesía Juglaresca y Juglares, Aspects of the history of the literature and culture of Spain, Madrid, 1924.

Floresta de Leyendas Heroicas Españolas, compiled by R. Menéndez Pidal.

Rodrigo, el último godo—Vol. I: "La Edad Media", Madrid, 1925.

Orígenes del Español. Estado Lingüístico de la Península Ibérica hasta el siglo XI, Madrid, 1926.

Flor Nueva de Romances Viejos, Madrid, 1928; 2nd ed. 1943.

La España del Cid, Madrid, 1929, 2 vols.

The Cid and his Spain, translated by H. Sunderland, Foreword by the Duke of Alba, London, 1934.

The following works of Menéndez Pidal have been reprinted in the Colección Austral, Madrid and Buenos Aires

De Cervantes y Lope de Vega—No. 120.

Antología de Prosistas Españolas—No. 110.

Poesía Árabe y Poesía Europea—No. 190.

Flor Nueva de Romanceros Viejos—No. 100.

Castilla, la Tradición y el Idioma—No. 501.

Idea Imperial de Carlos V—No. 172.

Estudios Literarios—No. 28.

El Idioma Español en sus Primeros Tiempos—No. 250.

Poesía Juglaresca y Juglares—No. 300.

Homenaje Ofrecido a Menéndez Pidal, 3 vols., Madrid, 1925.

IN THE NORTON LIBRARY

Beales, Derek. *From Castlereagh to Gladstone, 1815–1885.* N367

Bemis, Samuel Flagg. *The Latin American Policy of the United States.* N412

Benda, Julien. *The Treason of the Intellectuals.* N470

Billington, Ray Allen (editor) *The Reinterpretation of Early American History.* N446

Blair, Peter Hunter. *Roman Britain and Early England 55 B.C.–A.D. 871* N361

Bloch, Marc. *Strange Defeat: A Statement of Evidence Written in 1940.* N371

Bober, M. M. *Karl Marx's Interpretation of History.* N270

Brandt, Conrad. *Stalin's Failure in China.* N352

Brinton, Crane. *The Lives of Talleyrand.* N188

Brodie, Fawn. *Thaddeus Stevens.* N331

Brooke, Christopher. *From Alfred to Henry III, 871–1272.* N362

Brown, Roger H. *The Republic in Peril: 1812.* N578

Bury, J. B. et al. *The Hellenistic Age.* N544

Bushman, Richard L. *From Puritan to Yankee: Character and the Social Order in Connecticut, 1690–1765.* N532

Butterfield, Herbert. *The Whig Interpretation of History.* N318

Chadwin, Mark Lincoln. *The Warhawks: American Interventionists Before Pearl Harbor.* N546

Chang, Hsin-pao. *Commissioner Lin and the Opium War.* N521

Cobban, Alfred. *Aspects of the French Revolution.* N512

Collis, Maurice. *Foreign Mud: The Opium Imbroglio at Canton in the 1830's and the Anglo-Chinese War.* N462

Cornish, Dudley Taylor. *The Sable Arm: Negro Troops in the Union Army, 1861–1865.* N334

Dehio, Ludwig. *Germany and World Politics in the Twentieth Century.* N391

De Roover, Raymond. *The Rise and Decline of The Medici Bank.* N350

Dumond, Dwight Lowell. *Antislavery.* N370

Dunn, Richard S. *Puritans and Yankees: The Winthrop Dynasty of New England, 1630–1717.* N597

Embree, Ainslie T. (editor) *Alberuni's India.* N568

Erikson, Erik H. *Young Man Luther.* N170

Eyck, Erich. *Bismarck and the German Empire.* N235

Feis, Herbert. *Contest Over Japan.* N466

Ferrell, Robert H. *American Diplomacy in the Great Depression: Hoover-Stimson Foreign Policy, 1929–1933.* N511

Ferrell, Robert H. *Peace in Their Time: The Origins of the Kellogg-Briand Pact.* N491

Finley, M. I. *Early Greece: The Bronze and Archaic Ages.* N541

Franklin, John Hope. *The Free Negro in North Carolina, 1790–1860.* N579

Ganshof, Francois Louis. *Frankish Institutions Under Charlemagne.* N500

Gash, Norman. *Politics in the Age of Peel.* N564

Gatzke, Hans W. *Stresemann and the Rearmament of Germany.* N486

Gay, Peter. *The Party of Humanity: Essays in the French Enlightenment.* N607

Graves, Robert and Alan Hodge. *The Long Week-end: A Social History of Great Britain, 1918–1939.* N217

Greene, Jack P. *The Quest for Power: The Lower Houses of Assembly in the Southern Royal Colonies, 1689–1776.* N591

Halperin, S. William. *Germany Tried Democracy.* N280

Hamilton, Holman. *Prologue to Conflict.* N345

Haring, C. H. *Empire in Brazil.* N386

Haskins, Charles Homer. *The Normans in European History.* N342

Hill, Christopher. *The Century of Revolution 1603–1714.* N365

Holmes, George. *The Later Middle Ages, 1272–1485.* N363

Huizinga, Jan. *In the Shadow of Tomorrow.* N484

Jolliffe, J. E. A. *The Constitutional History of Medieval England.* N417

Keir, David Lindsay. *The Constitutional History of Modern Britain Since 1485.* N405

Kendall, Paul Murray. *The Yorkist Age.* N558

Kendall, Paul Murray (editor) *Richard III: The Great Debate.* N310

Kolko, Gabriel. *Railroads and Regulation, 1877–1916.* N531

Lamar, Howard Roberts. *The Far Southwest, 1846–1912.* N522

Leach, Douglass E. *Flintlock and Tomahawk: New England in King Philip's War.* N340

McFeely, William S. *Yankee Stepfather: General O.O. Howard and the Freedmen.* N537

Madison, James. *Notes of Debates in the Federal Convention of 1787.* N485

Magrath, C. Peter. *Yazoo: The Case of Fletcher v. Peck.* N418

Marwick, Arthur. *The Deluge: British Society and the First World War.* N523

Mattingly, Harold. *The Man in the Roman Street.* N337

Mattingly, Harold. *Roman Imperial Civilization.* N572

May, Arthur J. *The Hapsburg Monarchy: 1867–1914.* N460

Mosse, Claude. *The Ancient World at Work.* N540

Neale, J. E. *Elizabeth I and Her Parliaments,* 2 vols. N359a & N359b

Noggle, Burl. *Teapot Dome: Oil and Politics in the 1920's.* N297

North, Douglass C. *The Economic Growth of the United States 1790–1860.* N346

Ogilvie, R. M. *The Romans and Their Gods in the Age of Augustus.* N543

Pelling, Henry. *Modern Britain, 1885–1955.* N368

Pirenne, Henri. *Early Democracies in the Low Countries.* N565

Pollack, Norman. *The Populist Response to Industrial America.* N295

Quirk, Robert E. *The Mexican Revolution, 1914–1915.* N507

Read, Conyers. *The Tudors.* N129

Remini, Robert V. *Martin Van Buren and the Making of the Democratic Party.* N527

Ritcheson, Charles. *Aftermath of Revolution: British Policy Toward the United States, 1783–1795.* N553

Robson, Eric. *The American Revolution, 1763–1783.* N382

Roth, Cecil. *The Spanish Inquisition.* N255

Rowse, A. L. *Appeasement.* N139

Ruiz, Ramon Eduardo. *Cuba: The Making of a Revolution.* N513

Sarton, George. *A History of Science, I: Ancient Science Through the Golden Age of Greece.* N525

Sarton, George. *A History of Science, II: Hellenistic Science and Culture in the Last Three Centuries B.C.* N526

Seton-Watson, R. W. *Disraeli, Gladstone, and the Eastern Question.* N594

Smith, Abbot E. *Colonists in Bondage: White Servitude and Convict Labor in America, 1607–1776.* N592

Sontag, Raymond J. *Germany and England: Background of Conflict, 1848–1894.* N180

Spanier, John W. *The Truman-MacArthur Controversy and the Korean War.* N279

Stansky, Peter and William Abrahams. *Journey to the Frontier: Two Roads to the Spanish Civil War.* N509

Tan, Chester C. *The Boxer Catastrophe.* N575

Tarbell, Ida M. *History of the Standard Oil Company.* N496

Taylor, A. J. P. *Germany's First Bid for Colonies, 1884–1885.* N530

Thompson, J. M. *Louis Napoleon and the Second Empire.* N403

Tolles, Frederick B. *Meeting House and Counting House.* N211

Tourtellot, Arthur Bernon. *Lexington and Concord.* N194

Waite, Robert G. L. *Vanguard of Nazism: The Free Corps Movement in Postwar Germany, 1918–1923.* N181

Warmington, B. H. *Nero: Reality and Legend.* N542

Warren, Harris Gaylord. *Herbert Hoover and the Great Depression.* N394

Wedgwood, C. V. *William the Silent.* N185

Wheeler-Bennett, John W. *Brest-Litovsk: The Forgotten Peace, March 1918.* N576

Wolfers, Arnold. *Britain and France between Two Wars.* N343

Wolff, Robert Lee. *The Balkans in Our Time.* N395

Wright, Benjamin Fletcher. *Consensus and Continuity, 1776–1787.* N402

Zeldin, Theodore. *The Political System of Napoleon III.* N580

Zinn, Howard. *LaGuardia in Congress.* N488

Zobel, Hiller B. *The Boston Massacre.* N606